My Name Is Joe
And I Am a Pizza Man

An American Story

Copyright 2022 by Giuseppe Farruggio
All Rights Reserved

No part of this book may be reproduced or transmitted in any form or by any means, electronic or mechanical, including photocopying, recording, or by any information storage or retrieval system, without the prior written permission of the publisher, except in the case of brief quotations contained in reviews.

Front cover photo: Georgetown.com
Back cover illustration: Giancarlo Massimo Chiancone
Photos provided by the author.

Cover and book design: Richard Stodart

For permission to reproduce selections from this book, write to:

Fourth Lloyd Productions, LLC
512 Old Glebe Point Road
Burgess, VA 22432
USA

4thLloyd@gmail.com
https://richardstodart.com/publishing%3A-all-listings

ISBN: 978-1-7350341-5-7 paperback
ISBN: 978-1-7350341-6-4 ebook

Library of Congress Control Number: 2022914881

My Name Is Joe
And I Am a Pizza Man

An American Story

Joe Farruggio

with Thierry Sagnier

Fourth Lloyd Productions, LLC
Burgess, VA

Introduction

I've known Joe Farruggio for more than 30 years. I've rarely seen him without a smile, and I've never witnessed him refusing to help someone in need.

His ability to grasp the essentials of any situation quickly and, more important, accurately, is amazing. He has a knack for simplifying the complex, and this talent has served him well. Knowing him for all these years, I've watched him undergo changes and growth.

About a decade ago, I realized Joe is what American legends are made of. He came here really believing people were so well-off in the fabled United States that they didn't bother keeping the spare change from their purchases. He was told Americans threw their nickels, dimes, and quarters into the street, and from this assumption came his first business initiative. He would get up earlier than anyone else in Brooklyn, gather the discarded change, and get rich.

His success demanded a bit more work. Now, some fifty years after his arrival in New York, Joe has reaped the rewards of a half-century's work.

I'm proud to be his friend, and to have been given the opportunity to assist him in writing this book.

Thierry Sagnier, September 2021

One

Sicily is a small island with a big history. People have been living there for thousands of years, and it is now the most densely populated island in the Mediterranean Sea. Like the United States, it is a melting pot. Romans, Greeks, Trojans, Arabs, Normans, and more, have come there, left their marks on the Sicilian people, and then departed.

The Sicilians, of which I am one, have traditionally gone from their home to find better opportunities elsewhere. The town where I was born, Castrofilippo, used to have 6,500 people. Now it has 3,000. People leave; they go to other countries and set up their lives there, but they come back, like me, as often as they can. Sicily is the place of my birth, and it will always be my homeland. My heart is there.

I was born on June 28, 1953. My father, Rosario Farruggio, was a man of all trades and a farmer. My mother, Maria Asaro, gave birth to four of us: me, two brothers, and one sister. One brother, Dino, died after two weeks. My father had a first wife who gave him a son, Calogero, who everyone called Lillo. She later died in childbirth. My family was Lillo and Vincenzo, and my sister Maria. And then there was me, Giuseppe, the youngest. I was named after my uncle. My mother told me I was born on a rainy night in the house we lived in. All of us were born there, and all six of us lived in that little house.

I started to be aware of my life when I was probably six years old, when I'd be walking around with my father. My father was born in 1909; I was born in 1953, so there was a big age difference. I remember my father's friends used to make comments to him about me, like, "This boy is your crutch for your old age." They would say that, and I was sort of proud that I was his crutch, that I could help him, and that's pretty much the way it went. Even when I was older, I accompanied him all the time, to doctors and such. I was taking care of him for all the appointments that he needed over the years of my adulthood. When he passed away in 1988, I was there when he closed his eyes for the last time. I was the only one with him.

Everybody thought I was this wonderful little kid; that I was well behaved and sweet and quiet. And for some reason, I liked it, people believing that of me, but I wanted to be my own person.

Once I realized that people thought well of me, my life pretty much changed. I was maybe eight or nine years old, and a couple of years after this realization, I started smoking cigarettes. My friends and I used to look for butts in the streets and collect them, and then roll our own. Sometimes, when we were able to get 20 liras together, we could buy two cigarettes: one with the filter, one without. We'd smoke them and I remember feeling really, really dizzy, but at the same time, I liked it. I liked that it changed the way I was feeling.

I was smoking all alone since I was little. First, with butts from the street, and then by the time I was 16, I was a full smoker, one pack a day, but I hid it. I didn't want anybody to see it; I would hide my cigarettes. When I'd get home and smelled like tobacco, I'd tell my parents I'd been watching TV in the club where a lot of men were smoking.

We were a real farming family, but we didn't have much. There was some land where we used to cultivate our own food. We ate what we grew and traded or sold the rest. That was enough for us to live on. We had a female horse, and we had goats, rabbits, chickens, and we really didn't need anything at that time. The only thing we needed was sugar and salt; we used to buy those.

And those days, everybody traded family to family. We got cheese from the sheep man because he used to graze his sheep on our land, and at the end of the year, he'd give us five kilos of cheese, and that would last pretty much half a year. My mother used to make everything from *giardiniera* to tomato sauce and sundried tomatoes for the winter. Really, we didn't need very much from the store except the things that we couldn't make and really wanted, like candy and chocolates. They always looked so good, but most of the time I didn't have money to buy things like that.

The truth is, we barely earned enough money to feed the family. And I mean, barely; let's say, one year if it didn't rain enough on the farm, there was not enough wheat or fruit to sell, and we had to tighten our belts. I remember the desperation of my father when there was a bad year; he was concerned about how to survive. After you sell the beans, the almonds, the wheat, you sell the chickpeas, and you sell the milk from the goat. Every morning, you get two liters of milk and sell one liter. If you have 20 eggs, you sell 10 eggs, you know? If you have a rabbit or a chicken to sell, you sell it and you don't eat meat. The food was there, but we couldn't afford it.

I remember going to the pastry shop where they had a beautiful dessert that people came to buy, but we couldn't. You'd go to the butcher store and there was meat, but the meat that we bought, it was the cheapest cut. I thought that was normal because that's the level of poverty I grew up with. But we ate healthy; it was good food. It wasn't because the meat cut was bad that it cost less; it was actually even better because it was around the bone and had more flavor. My mother, she was a good cook. She knew how to feed us and cook for the family every night with soup, with meat or no meat, or beans with vegetables; there was always food at night.

There was a village press for the olives; with the wine, it was the same thing. You made your own wine, pressed your own olives. You picked the grapes and took them to the grape press and you either paid with wine or you paid with money. With the oil, it was the same thing. The people at the press did the work, and you'd give them a percentage of the oil or, if you could afford it, you paid with cash.

It was a lot of work on the farm. Sometimes, if it rained too much, a piece of land might get flooded, and we'd have to reroute the water. We were barely earning a living and not able to save anything.

My village at the time, it had about 6,500 people, with a mayor, and if you got sick, two or three doctors. There was kindergarten, elementary school, and junior high. But the high school was in another town. The kindergarten was where the nuns were. Now, in kindergarten, the buses pick the children up; but there was no buses before, back when I was a boy.

Some of the families, they'd let the kids stay with the nuns, so they could eat there until they were old enough and go on to elementary school and walk to school. Five years of elementary school, and then it was three years of middle school. And then after that, we went to another town, and we had to take the bus.

I had a good group of friends, and we used to hang around the neighborhood together. The town was split into four zones, and we used to have our own wars, our own games there. I really thought that the entire world was just the same, like my neighborhood.

And then, when I was around 10 years old, in 1963, my uncle, who had left Italy and lived in America, in New York, he came to Sicily. What I remember is that he was talking to my dad, and he said, "What are you going to do with those kids? Why don't you take them off the farm and bring them to America? Come to America with us."

My uncle described America like it was a candy store and a toy store, and that you could find money in the street; he told us that people threw the change away when they bought something. They were so rich, they didn't bother to keep it. And I heard this, and in my mind when he said it was, "Wow! I can get up early and I'll go walk around the streets and pick up all those pennies, and then I'll go to the store and exchange them for bills, and that will be pretty much all I'll need to do. I'll eat candy and cakes, and I'll have a lot of toys!"

And this was important because I never had toys of my own until my older brother Lillo went into the military and bought me a toy police car. That was the first toy I ever got. I was probably six or seven years old.

I remember my uncle saying, "You got to take them out of the dirt, take them off the farm and bring them to America. I'll do all the necessary paperwork and sponsorship."

There wasn't any discussion about it, not that I remember. I only know I was told I was going to go to America.

We didn't talk in the family. I never talked to my dad, maybe sometimes to my mom. Talking about your problems, it wasn't done. It wasn't something I would do. I don't think anybody did that. If you had something wrong and somebody else noticed, maybe you could get help. If you didn't, it would pass.

Anyway, after my uncle and my dad decided, I started dreaming about America.

In my town, everybody emigrates. They go all over the world, Germany, France, England. Half of them go to America. The ones that come to America, they never go back to Sicily to live. But if they go to Germany or France, one third of them go back. But 99 percent of the people that come to America, they stay. They come back for vacation, maybe, like I do, or to see family. But once they're in America, that's it.

People from my town, Castrofilippo, are everywhere. In my town, if nobody had left, we could have been 10, maybe 12,000 by now. Out of 6,500 people there, a lot came to New York.

I mean, it was an opportunity for my father. He was pretty old to become an immigrant at the time; he was 53 when he made that decision. Then he had to wait for the immigration people to do all the paperwork, so when we came to America, he was 61 years old. I was almost 17. My brother Vinny was 19, and mom was 51. My oldest brother, Lillo, didn't want to come, and my sister, Maria, was over 21, so she had to wait an extra six months.

That discussion between my father and my uncle, and the realization we were going to America, that pretty much changed my view of life, once again.

When my uncle came back to Sicily, I was around 10, and now for the second time, the world opened up in my imagination, and I realized that I was not going to be in that little town forever, that someday, eventually, I was going to leave Sicily. I was going to go to America. But it took a long time. All the paperwork had to be done, and this was before computers or emails. My uncle was sponsoring us, and there were interviews and meetings, and forms to fill and send, so we could get green cards for the family. And so, between 10 to about 16-and-a-half, I pretty much changed. I continued evolving.

I was a very insecure, very shy kid. That was how I saw myself, but when I was around my friends, I was rebellious and funny, and I was a bully, too. I started fights with other kids, sometimes much bigger boys than me, and didn't mind getting hit; I didn't mind the pain. What I liked was the idea that I was getting attention. People would notice me. My friends, they'd say, "Wow! You won!" Stuff like that.

But at the same time, I was growing up and in school, well, I was really bad at school. When I showed up at school for the first grade, I was really shy, and I didn't feel like I was dressed right; I didn't have new shoes, and my pants were patched. I saw a few other kids who were worse off than me, and a few other kids that were better off than me. And then, I realized we were mixing together; the rich kids and the poor kids were all in one class with one teacher.

In my town at that time, with so few people living there, everybody knew each other, but there were different class levels. My family, we were not in the lowest; we were probably in the middle. Our house had three rooms. In the main room, we had my father and my mother's bed. Under the stairs, there was another tiny area where me and my brothers slept. And then, we had this bed that opened up next to the dining table, where my sister slept. My oldest brother slept in the other room, which was supposed to be the living room, but it was just for looks. We had the radio there.

We had the horse and the goats and the rabbits in the room with an oven, and we fed the stove there with wood. There was always something cooking.

Oh, by the way, we didn't have a bathroom in my house because there was no sewer. So we went to the bathroom in the same room where we kept the horse and the goats. I'd poop in the same place the horse was pooping.

Sometimes we'd go outside of town. There was this old farmhouse where the electricity came in and there was an open entrance. Behind that, nobody could see, and everybody used that area for a bathroom. If you forgot your newspaper for toilet paper, you had to look around for a rock. If you were lucky, it might have rained, and the rock would be clean.

About a year before we left, that's when we got the sewer line to our house, and we got a bathroom. We had a bucket of water next to it, so we could empty water into the toilet to flush it.

Like I said before, we always had a meal at night; my mother would cook every night. Some of the time, the meal was quiet, but a lot of times, there was shouting and chaos with my brothers fighting each other.

During the meal, I got my plate, ate my portion, and then quickly went outside to where my friends lived, and whistled. That was how we signaled each other. They'd come out and we'd spend three, four hours together stealing fruit, getting into movies and watching TV, or throwing fireworks and fighting and playing jokes and games.

Hanging out with my friends, there was a lot of wish talk, but not real talk. At night when I went out with them, we'd decide not to go to school the next day and go catch butterflies instead, and I did, you know? So, those friends weren't better, education-wise, they were worse.

We had a whistle that when blown, maybe someone would come out and say, "Ten minutes," or, "I can't get out tonight because I've got to study," or there were other things going on and they couldn't come out and play.

There was this friend of mine, Rosario. He always had to do his homework first, then he had to wash up because his parents wanted him to look decent to go out. I didn't have all those rules. I could have been filthy; I didn't want to change; I went out the way I was. But this other guy, he had to clean up. He didn't go to the farm to work there, he didn't have a goat, he didn't have to do all that, so he would stay clean.

I thought other families lived better than I did, and so going to my first school, I just felt *so* uncomfortable. There were a few kids who were a lot more advanced than me. I didn't know anything, and I pretty much closed up. Anyway, they passed me for the first grade. I didn't pass the second grade for two years.

In June, after school ended, we went to live in the countryside. One of my uncles leased the farm to my dad. We would spend the summer there until the end of August, basically planting and taking care of the land and picking the crops.

Over there, I was pretty much on my own. I had a dog, but she didn't live with us in town. We left her at the farm during the rest of the year. That dog, she was my best friend. She was my companion, and we went everywhere together.

Her name was Giulia. Since I was little, we've always had a dog. When we came to America, we actually had one, but dogs weren't like the way you know them today. Here in the U.S., you let them in the house, give them a pedicure, and bathe them. In Sicily, dogs, they were working animals, and they stayed outside all year long.

Giulia, she was a watchdog. She was living at the farm, and she guarded it. In the summertime, she was always with me. Everything I did, she would come with me.

The one thing I remember with the dog is that, when I went back to Sicily three or four years after I left for America, I went to the street where my farm was, and the dog was still there.

She remembered me; it just blew me away. By then, I was older, and seeing how dogs were getting treated in America, I felt guilty. But when I was a kid, it wasn't in my power to change things. I was young, and that's the way the culture was.

Anyway, during the winter, I would feed her. I went once a day, every day. I had this container that I put leftovers in, and I'd go to the farm. There was a bowl there, and I would dump everything in it and leave. And a lot of times, because the weather was bad and it rained or it was cold and I didn't want to walk all the way there, I would call her, "Hey, Giulia!" She'd come running, and I'd feed her then and there. Then I'd tell her to go back to the farm.

We were at the farm the entire summer; I remember working all day, and it was hard work. My parents woke up very early before the sun came up and went to work. I'd get up with my brothers a little bit later and do was what was needed: harvesting tomatoes and weeding, trying to clean up the grasses here and there, so we could grow our beautiful vegetables. We worked until nine or nine-thirty in the morning; then it would get too hot, so we'd go inside or cool off under the trees, have lunch around noon, and take a siesta from one until about four. Then we'd work some more until about nine o'clock at night. We're talking about four hours in the morning, four hours in the evening, and then, dinner. After that was the best part of the day. We'd sit, and if there was an older person, they'd tell us stories. Those stories, for me, they were like watching the movies! They were creative, and they opened all sorts of fantasies.

So I worked on the farm from when I was very young; I was forced to do the same thing everybody else did. That was from when I was six or seven years old until we came to America,

And then there was my older brother Lillo. He was much older than the rest of us, and he pretty much ran the family. So what I wanted was to eat and get out of the house as soon as possible and be with my friends and be funny and rebellious. We'd spend the night ringing people's doorbells and then running away, and the people would open the door and scream like hell at us. Sometimes, we used to put a chicken cage on top of the front door, so, when they opened the door, the cage would fall on them. People used to get really, really pissed off, but we thought it was funny.

And that was pretty much the way those days went. Nothing much happened. People worked their entire lives, worked hard, and then they died.

In Castrofilippo, just like anywhere else, a few people died every month. When they did, within 24 hours they had to be taken to the cemetery. The bodies were never embalmed, like they are in the

U.S. Before the burial, there was a wake where all the family and friends would stop by and visit the dead.

They had the dead person in a room, sometimes the living room, depending on what kind of house they had. Some who had small houses put the bodies in the kitchen. They had a bed with a blanket, and they'd put the dead person in the middle of the room in the bed, and everybody would be dressed in black, sitting around on chairs and mumbling, talking about how the dead person had lived, and how they remembered this or that. In the family, the husband or the daughter or the son, they were in the middle, the central spot, and everybody would stand for ten minutes or half-an-hour and say prayers and say goodbye to the dead.

The children didn't go to the wake. The adults would go pay a visit, but the kids wouldn't unless it was a member of your family. My father's parents, they were already dead when I was born, so I didn't have much experience with death, except one time when the father of a friend died. I barely remember, but I know it happened.

For the first twenty-four hours, the body stayed in the house because they could not take it to the cemetery before that. Then they would go to church; everybody was Catholic. Four people would carry the casket into the church, and there would be a mass.

After that, they'd go to the cemetery, which was really chilling for me to see. They'd carry the body in the *carretto*, which originally was a horse-drawn cart. Later on, it would be a hearse.

The cemetery was less than a kilometer from the church, so there would be the hearse, then the family lined up behind that, and then all the other people. They'd put the casket in the Catholic chapel in the cemetery, and everybody would stand around and say goodbye to the family and leave.

I remember when funerals happened, when they were walking from the church to the cemetery, people would close the windows and the blinds in their houses. If they were outside talking, they'd go inside and close the door. Everything would be quiet. All the storefronts would close their doors when the mourners passed by. It was in respect for the dead.

Me and my friends, we'd watch the funerals go by. Where we lived was not too far from the cemetery. I was scared of burials.

Things change, though. My father passed away here in the United States.

He had a stroke, he didn't last long, about a week. I'd had a pretty good relationship with him, but I never really expressed it with words. I always found it difficult to say that I loved my father. When I was a kid, we never talked much. We got closer in the U.S.

The night before he passed, I was at the hospital with him, and my then-wife said, "I don't think your dad looks like he's going to make it much longer." She told me, "You should stay here."

I couldn't tell that it was that bad. He didn't look as if he was going to die. My father was there all my life, so I didn't think he was ever going to be gone. So I stayed, and about nine or ten o'clock that night, he started breathing hard, like it was difficult for him to get air. I was sitting next to him. I held his hand, and I told him I loved him. A couple hours after that, he took his last breath and passed away.

His last wish was to go back to Italy. He had told his brother that if he died first, he wanted him to get a band for the funeral. So he was embalmed here in Virginia, and we put him in this beautiful casket. But to get the documents required to take him back to Italy, it was incredibly difficult.

During the '80s, Sicily was known for the Mafia, with drugs; there was a lot of that going on, and the drug people, they used caskets to bring the drugs in and out. So it took two weeks for us to get everything cleared up. Meanwhile, my dad was at the funeral home. After they gave us the permission, me and my brother, we travelled with the casket to Sicily. It was very emotional to go to our hometown and accompany my father, who was in the back of the funeral car. We were in a separate car, and we took him straight to the church from the airport.

We got to the church, and I told my cousin, who was one of the doctors of the town, that we're going to have an open casket. And he says, "Are you crazy? How can you open it two weeks after his death?"

I said, "No, it's fine." I got the funeral people to open the casket. I had to fix my father because he had moved a little bit; they must have bumped into something, and his position was a little bit bent. With my bare hands, I took my father and I moved him into place, and my cousin is like, "Don't touch him!" Because, you know, he was going to fall apart. But I fixed my father; I was really close to him, I had no problem doing that, it was natural for me.

Also, right after the mass, the family went to another room next to the church, the sacristy. All the people that were in the church came and shook your hands or gave you a kiss. For me, it was like a movie. I'd see all those faces, and by then I'd lived in America almost 18 years, since 1970. People had gotten older; they knew my father, and they'd come to pay their respects. Family and strangers, our neighbors, everybody. The same thing happened years later when my mom passed away.

With my father, it was really, really beautiful, because there was a car, there was us: me, my brothers, my sister, uncles, and cousins. There was the band with funeral music. We took him to the cemetery like everybody else, and that was it. I like to think it's what my father wanted.

But when I was a kid back in Sicily, we avoided the cemetery. It scared us.

Two

In Castrofilippo, there was nothing interesting to do except be with my friends.

The politicians of the town had clubs with a TV. In those days, there were only Channel One and Channel Two.

At nine o'clock, there would be a show, *Carosello,* with advertisements which everybody would love to see. They were selling products we didn't even recognize; these were all new things for us—dishwashers and washing machines and liquors and beers we'd never heard of. And so, we would rush to watch those ads, and then, because we liked to think we were rebels, they'd kick us out because we were making noise, joking, singing, and the older people didn't want us there. To get revenge, we used to retaliate.

I remember one time I went to buy some firecrackers. When we had them, we tried to get into this club with a TV; it was mostly full of old people. They used to smoke and watch TV. Sometimes, they didn't let me in, sometimes, they did. One day, I said, "Okay, you're not going to let me in?" The window was open because they wanted to let the smoke out, and I threw the firecrackers inside the TV club room. That got their attention, but they knew that it was me and after that I couldn't go back to that place. They knew I'd done it, but they couldn't prove it.

There was this guy from another town who was selling fruits with a Lambretta three-wheeler, and me and my friend Angelo, when the man got in to go from one street to another, we went in the back and got a big bunch of bananas and took off running. We ran and ran and went to the farm; we would hide there eating bananas like we were champions. We stashed some of them and went back later. And when we went back to town, the ladies on the street who'd seen us, because they saw everything, they told the guy who we were.

"Oh, that was Giuseppe and Angelo!"

When we got home that night, it was like, "What did you do?"

"Well, nothing."

"What do you mean, nothing? Who got the bananas?"

"What bananas? I never did anything."

Our parents ended up paying for the bananas.

Anyway, that was pretty much what we did. At night, we'd entertain ourselves by stealing from the *bottega*, which was a little store where they sold essentials. They used to bring cases of orange, bananas, apples, and keep them outside at nighttime. Me and my friends, we'd make sure the owner was serving a customer, and we'd steal a couple of apples, or oranges, and bananas.

And that was the only time I got to eat a banana, when I stole it; they were very expensive and not in our budget.

We used to play a lot of games. My friends, they were all interested in girls; they all liked somebody. But me, I was very, very shy; I did not know how to get close to a girl. In my mind, I used to build a lot of scenarios of how I was going to propose to this girl that I really liked, Rosetta. One time I decided I was going to give her a present; I bought a pen and gave it to her, but I don't remember if she accepted it or not. Probably not.

Rosetta, yeah. When I came back to Castrofilippo the second time in the mid '70s, there was a priest in my church. He was a sort of an idealistic guy, and he pulled a lot of young people together and it became a political movement. A new generation of the town was with him, and then he changed. He took off his priest collar, and he became a mayor of the town. Rosetta married him. I went back to Italy; I saw her a couple of times, but I don't think she ever recognized me.

Anyway, we used to go walk around with my friends in the streets where the girls lived. My friends were a little more advanced than me in that department. Or at least I thought they were. That was pretty much that.

I had a bicycle that my two brothers had used. By the time it got to me, it was really old and busted, so I repaired it. And then later on, I had a little moped that went through my two brothers, too. By the time it got to me, it was in pretty bad shape, too. But I couldn't wait to get it, you know, the moped, and I destroyed it even more.

At our farm, we were growing lettuce, tomatoes, onions, zucchini, eggplant, and other vegetables. And we also had this tree of *gelsi*, mulberries in English, that would be mature in June. My father started making me sell this stuff in town when I was still very young.

Really, I didn't like it, but I did it because I had this sense that I had to make some income for the family. I used the bicycle to carry the vegetables and sell them on the street. I was embarrassed when my friends would see me, but I was not embarrassed with the ladies. They used to call on me, and I had a scale, and I would weigh the vegetables and calculate the cost. That would last for about two hours in the morning.

I started with the *gelsis*; that was the first crop of the season. I used to sell them for 15 lira, and I remember making 300, 400 lira from one bush. Those weighed about 10 kilos, and at the end of a couple of hours, I'd make good money, and I liked that, making money. I kept a little, maybe 50 lira every time. And that was enough to buy a *panino* at night. It was great: I had money, and my friends didn't, though some of them got money from their parents.

I also used the bicycle to sell the zucchini, string beans, and *tenerumi*. *Tenerumi* are the leaves of the squash plants, and you use them to cook pasta. I did that until I came to America. I was known in Castrofilippo for being the kid that was selling the best *gelsis* and vegetables.

We used to organize parties, me and my friends, all boys, maybe five, six of us. They each had their own personality, and they came from different backgrounds. One of them was learning to be a mechanic, the other ones helped their fathers in the farms. At that time, my best friend was Rosario, and he was always dressed nicer than anybody else. He was, and still is, my best friend.

The first time I got drunk was for Carnival in February. It was like Halloween. I dressed up as a soldier; I don't remember how everybody else was dressed up. But we were knocking on doors, and every house we went to, they were offering us candy or a glass of wine, and every time, I picked the wine. Sometimes, I got some Marsala, which is very dry and sweet and native to Sicily. I chose the alcohol all the time. That night, I got so drunk, when I got home, my parents were terrified. They put me on top of the dining room table, trying to sober me up. My whole body was paralyzed. I remember seeing everybody really clearly. I was hearing a lot of background noise, but my vision was clear, and I was thinking, "Why are they worried about me? I'm here!" I couldn't figure out why they were concerned. So I went to sleep, and the next day, I didn't think anything of it.

I drank at San Martino, which is the holiday when you kill the pig and drink the wine. And then, it was for *Pasquetta*, the day after Easter.

We also used to get together with friends and cook; we'd have three hundred lira each and buy potatoes and cheap meat.

We'd go to an empty farmhouse, my parents', or somebody else's. We were just boys, but we cooked some beautiful meals, and there was always, wine, and I'd get really drunk again.

I didn't know what alcoholism was. That came much later. There were about four or five older men—you never saw any women—they were lower class and were always at the *locanda* drinking wine. They went there to drink, maybe eat some tripe, pig's feet, or sausage, and drink wine. Since we didn't have a television, we were going into the political clubs to watch TV there. At the end, around ten o'clock at night, you'd see those guys, always the same people, drunk and going home. They didn't disturb anybody. Almost nobody was giving them work, and when they were working, it was for less than everybody else. They would do a lot of odd jobs, "Oh, you have to paint this wall," or, "You want me to remove this dirt?" They were unemployed, and they drank a lot. That's what I knew about drunks.

One time in town, we planned a dance with my friend. Rosario organized parties to invite girls, and adults were there too, of course. At that time, I liked this girl, but I didn't know how to approach her. Anyway, this was the first time I asked a girl to dance, a slow dance, and I don't know if it was the wine or if it was because I was holding the girl in my arms, but I was flying. I felt the best I ever felt in my life.

By the end of the night, I got so drunk that I remember this friend putting a bottle in my mouth and I was drinking it. He was also young, and after that, I really never trusted him as much anymore because he wanted me to get even drunker than I already was.

My father had a garage where we kept my brother's car, and we used to keep wine casks there. Now, I don't know if it was my idea or somebody else's, but someone said, "Wow, you have wine! Let's drink some wine!" We'd put a hose inside a cask and suck out the wine. There again, I got drunk pretty bad.

But you know, all those times, I didn't think anything of it. I never thought I really did that much drinking, other than with my friends or sometimes when there was a wedding in town.

If somebody got married, at the entrance of the banquet hall, they had a round table with a bunch of little shots of alcohol. They'd fill the glasses with homemade alcohol, all different colors. It wasn't strong, more like a vermouth. When the guests came in, a member of the family would walk them to where the bride and the groom were. Me and my friends, we'd sneak in there and drink a couple of shots very fast and run away. We'd do that until we got a little buzz, but we could not get away with it for too long. Somebody in the wedding would notice. That was another way we all drank together, with my friends. But it was normal, you know, boys having fun is all it was.

Then, as I grew older, there were four or five of us, going to each neighborhood at night to walk around and make noise, so the girls would know we were outside. We really never went out and did things with the girls, because in the '60s, the girls were untouchable.

We didn't have sex; it was not even an idea. What the boys would do was, during the holidays when everybody was mixed, they'd go behind a woman and you know, maybe brush against her, stuff like that.

But really, most of the time, there were never any women; it was all boys. Girls were not allowed to come; they would get together among themselves, and boys among themselves, too; no mixing. Girls were very scarce. It was like, "Wow, you saw above the knees?" When I came here to the U.S., I thought I was in a candy store. I became like a Casanova here! I learned the game; you could pick up a girl anywhere.

I remember that in Castrofilippo, we were doing a bunch of

fighting; a lot of bullying and fighting with other kids. Sometimes you'd sneak into a movie theater by breaking the back doors.

By the time I was 12 or 13, the family had the Lambretta three-wheel scooter with cargo space in the back for deliveries. My brother had a car, a Fiat 600, and I used to get in the car and drive it back and forth inside the garage, or I'd start it, shift, and ride it—never far from the house. Sometimes, I'd take the Lambretta and ride around town.

A few years before I came to America, Lillo bought a Volkswagen truck. He started his own business selling dry goods, lentils, beans, nuts, and dates, going to every town's market. He made a lot of money. He did really well.

I would sneak into his truck. There was a wood box where he kept all the change from his sales, and that was one source to get money. I didn't steal too much, just enough, maybe 500 lira, 800 lira, depending on what I needed the money for. I never got caught.

There was one time when me and a friend stole a motorcycle. His family had a business, so he'd go into the cash drawer, steal money from the parents, and one day he asked, "You want to come with me?"

We were walking, and there was this motorcycle in the grass on the side of the road. People were probably working at the farm, and they'd left the motorcycle laying there.

We started it and began driving. I sat on the back, and we went to the next village 10 miles away. We kept that motorcycle at some friend's house until we ran out of gas. We were 13, something like that. I don't remember what we did with the cycle after that. Maybe we just left it on the side of the road.

We stole eggs. And one time, me and my cousin, we decided to go steal some sunflowers. I said, "Let's go, they'll be ours." I didn't know what I was going to do with the sunflowers because everybody grew them. Stealing some was a thing that boys did. In cherry season, we'd steal cherries. I would go with four or five kids, climb the trees, break some of the branches and eat the cherries.

There was one afternoon when the owner was under a tree sleeping, and then he saw us and started running after us and throwing rocks. He almost hit me, and I thought, "If I get hit in the head, it's going to kill me!" And the guy, I know he recognized us, who we were, so I'm running and running and running away, and I went to hide behind a farmhouse. My cousin, he went to our farm, where my mother and my brother were, and he said, "Yeah, we got caught…" I was so scared, I stayed hidden. About five, six hours later, my family came and got me.

I was in trouble a lot. One day we were picking grapes to make wine on my uncle's farm. We used the Lambretta three-wheeler, and we went to help my uncle take the grapes to the wine press. The Lambretta was very full, and we had to push it to get it off of the land and on to the main road. My brother told me I had to walk, but I didn't want to, so I sat hiding in the back of the three-wheeler, and my brother drove. And then, once we got to the highway, I got scared. I thought, "If he catches me…"

The Lambretta was probably going 30 kilometers an hour, and I jumped off and hit the pavement and fainted. I got all banged up and scratched, and a car stopped to help me out. It could have hit me. I was really hurting. I told them I was all right and walked by myself to the farm, and I went to the attic and hid for hours. I didn't tell anybody what I'd done; I was all bruised up, and they didn't know.

One time, I had to go to the farm, and I didn't want to. I wanted to go meet my friends. My parents had to go work and my father asked me to go get water for them from the terracotta jar. And because I was so angry at having to work, I peed in the jar.

We went back to the countryside every summer. I used to wear no shoes or socks, just a pair of shorts. I felt like Tarzan because I used to know all of the surrounding area, and I was okay walking around by myself with my dog. I knew what fruit was going to be ripe, and I'd pick the fruit, even if the tree wasn't on my land. But I knew I was stealing, and sometimes I felt a little bad about it, but it was not a big deal, really.

We gave a goat to the local sheep and goat man around June and got her back in September or October when she was pregnant. It was my job to feed it and to provide for it. And that became another animal friend; we spent a lot of time together. She was stubborn; I used to bully her. Today, we'd consider it animal abuse, but the goat didn't want to listen to me, and she used to run away from me. We had fresh goat milk through the whole winter, and we sold it. We had milk all the time. I milked the goat in the morning; my mother did it in the afternoon. We milked it into an aluminum container with a metal handle. We'd hang it off the ground and, in the morning, we would have buttercream. I'd get a piece of bread, and it was a race with my brothers and sister to see whoever got to the buttercream first, because it was a real treat! My mom would warm up the milk, put in two spoons of coffee so it got some color. We didn't use sugar because it was too expensive. Instead, we put on salt and ate it with hard bread; that was our breakfast.

Once in a while, we used to buy a container of ricotta, and it was the same thing; you put the hard bread in the container and mixed it. It was delicious! It was like a holiday for me!

When we went to *campagnia*, my breakfast depended on the season. If there were cherries, I'd climb the tree and have my breakfast there. If there were figs, me and my siblings would climb the fig tree, or peach tree, whatever there was we could pick. For lunch, my mother asked me to get vegetables for the minestrone. We had this beautiful minestrone! It was delicious, but I hated it sometimes because it was the same thing for the whole summer. We'd put in *tenerumi,* zucchini*, cavoli,* and beans, and potatoes, onions, olive oil, and we ate it with *ditalini* pasta; the same, the same, the same. Then on Sunday, we'd have the same pasta with tomato sauce, which was my favorite.

Once a year, at the end of the summer, beginning of September, we'd go to the city, Agrigento.

My father and I, my mother and my brothers and sister, all of us went except my older brother Lillo. My parents would go shopping for the clothes we needed to go back to school, and shoes and dresses, and the necessities for the holidays. All the other clothes we wore regular days, we bought them on Sunday in our own village. There were people that came and sold used clothes and used shoes, shirts, and pants, and stuff. My mother went to buy things there, and that's what we wore every day. But on Sunday, of course, we were dressed up a little bit better with the clothes bought in Agrigento. On the way back home, after we finished shopping, my father would buy Sicilian pizza. It was out of this world! Even now that I'm in the family pizza business, I'll never be able to make the same pizza; that's how good it was. It was a once-a-year thing, a real treat! Then we went home.

Three

Back in town, there was *La Festa della Madonna*, in September. That's when we got to dress up. There was music and fireworks, and there was a market where they sold cakes and prepared foods, and there'd be toys and music. At the feast, it was a beautiful, beautiful feeling, and we'd wait the whole year for the holiday and for the feast.

In Castrofilippo, there were five holidays that meant something. The important ones were *Festa di Sant'Antonio, Festa di Santa Lucia, Festa della Madonna, Natale,* which is Christmas, and *Pasqua,* Easter. These were the holidays that we would celebrate by getting dressed up and going to mass. It was also when we got to spot girls. They would get dressed up and go to church.

Sant'Antonio was some time in June, *Santa Lucia* was in December, *La Madonna* was in September. Those were the days when we had a better-than-average meal with larger servings of meat and sweets.

Then there was August 15. That was like the Fourth of July in America, and we usually were in the country house. And when I say country house, I don't mean it was luxurious. I mean the farmhouse where we worked. What I like about that memory is that on August 14 at night, we would make things out of dried grass in the shape of houses, or bicycles, or cars, things we'd want to get eventually, and we'd wait until it was really dark, and we'd light them on fire. The next morning, the ashes would be in the shape of a house, car, or whatever we'd designed.

As I got older, 13, 14, I'd collect almonds. The people who grew them got the almonds out of the trees when they were ready to be harvested. They'd miss some of them, and I'd pick them up, a few every day of the season, until maybe I got 10 kilos, which I'd sell. That was my money for the holiday, and I could buy whatever I wanted with it.

And then, school started. When we went back, I didn't pass second grade, I repeated second grade for two years. The third year, I passed. So, that made me older than the average age in the class. I remember when I was in third grade, our teacher put us in groups to study.

The teacher was the mayor of the town. He was a good mayor. I mean, he was really working for the town, but he was also drinking and playing cards at night at the café and doing his political thing. And when he came to class, he would just fall asleep. In the third, fourth, and fifth grade, we learned zero; we had no basis for going to the middle school. We loved it because we got to do whatever we wanted. We were playing and fighting and making noise, but he was sleeping; he couldn't hear us. Ten minutes before the bell rang, he would wake up and say, "Okay guys, this is the lesson. Do this for tomorrow." I never touched the books, and I'm sure more than half the class did the same thing.

It was a different story when we got to middle school. In fourth and fifth grade, there was a lot of bullying going on, and I was a little shy, but I did not take any abuse from anybody. So, I would rebel and started a lot of fights. That was going on almost on a weekly basis.

I had nice group of friends. My best friend was Rosario, and my other best friend was Lillo Cammilleri. Rosario was very creative and very open. Lillo, I always thought, was a follower, even though he wanted to win all the time. He wanted to lead, but we didn't let him. There were other kids. Some of them are already gone; they died of natural causes. And there was one who was a suicide. He was an alcoholic and had some mental illness. Another friend became captain of the *Polizia di Palermo*, and then he died in a car accident. Others, like my cousin Luigi Farruggio, died of stomach cancer.

Oh man, we were rebellious in the class! There was this guy, he later became a friend too. His parents had a business, and he always had money in his pocket. By that time, I had my moped, and he loved to ride it, so I'd get money from him to buy gas. I'd let him ride it, and he would fill up my tank.

We were rebelling. There were a few times in middle school when my schoolmates attacked the teachers. The teachers were not in control; we were in control of the class. We had this female teacher who was really nice, but she couldn't manage us. There was all kinds of stuff going on in that class.

When I graduated, the teacher told my parents, "Really, Giuseppe, he should not pass. I'll pass him, but you need to pay attention to him." I passed because the principal was a friend of my father. My father talked to me, and I promised him I'd go to the equivalent of high school and that I'd do better.

High school was in another town, Canicattì, about 10 kilometers away, and we had to ride the bus, but the bus pass was almost 950 lira per week. My father gave me 950 lire, and I would hitchhike to school. My friends and I would buy *panino* with the money.

Rosario was in the same school, but he was studying geometry, and I was in accounting. We'd travel together all the time, hitch-hiking. Our teachers would see us walking home, and they'd give us a lift. And then, we would go and buy lunch. We were starving because by the time we got back home, it was two o'clock, and we'd left for school at seven in the morning.

Often, we'd stay in Canicatti, which was a bigger place; that town had 40,000 people, and there were some good stores. We'd go look at the windows and see the things that we liked. I was 15, and I didn't want to have my parents buy my clothes; I wanted to buy my own, because they always bought me stuff that could last me a couple of years. I was growing. They'd buy stuff with long sleeves, long pants, always a little bit bigger than I needed. And I said no because I was looking at what was the style. I'd take my mother and my sister to the stores I liked and made sure my father didn't come.

Back in Castrofilippo there was a lot of other stuff like sneaking into the movie theater. There was one movie theater in my village, and we'd be begging the older people to give us a little money, so we could buy a ticket. A lot of times, we'd hide behind the coats of the adults and sneak in. I didn't think it was bad, I thought it was great, really. I was having fun because it was a challenge. It was always a challenge to get what I wanted, to do what I wanted to do. It didn't matter if I didn't have the money; I wanted to be like everybody else. I never missed anything because I always got in, one way or the other.

In the fall of 1969, we received a letter that all the paperwork by the U.S. Immigration people was done. We were going to go to America! All those years, waiting for the paperwork to come through, I had that notion in the back in my mind, that I was going to go to America. When we finally got the papers, my fantasy pretty much cut loose! I told all my friends! I was already in school and continued school until Christmas, and then, I started going to work with my brother, Lillo, with his truck. I worked for free; I was taking all the money I needed when he wasn't looking, and I continued to do that. I didn't feel bad; he didn't give me any money, so I was getting my own pay!

I did that in January and February. Then, for the first time, I went to Palermo.

It was amazing for me. Palermo was *big*, a big city with buildings! I saw buildings, I saw roads, they had sewers, and there were city boutiques. I was thinking, "Geez, what is it going to be like in America if Palermo's like that?"

We went to the American consulate. At the time, there were investigators, and if you were associated with any political party, like the Communists, you couldn't get the visa. But we passed the tests, and then we did the physical.

Then it was time for the family to get ready. My father got the boat tickets for all of us, except for my older brother, Lillo. He didn't want to come to America. He'd gotten married a week before we left. And then it turned out my sister Maria would have to wait six months. She had just turned 21, and the American law apparently said she was an adult, and she couldn't come with us right away.

The day before we got on the boat, we went to the public showers, because we didn't have any showers at home. We'd clean up using buckets. You'd wash your feet, and somebody threw water on you, and you'd wash the rest of yourself. That was the first time I had a real shower; I was 16.

The next day, we got up very early, drove to Palermo, and took the ferry to Naples and boarded the ship, the *Michelangelo*. My uncle came from Rome to Naples to see us off.

I remember the separation, and I remember the night before leaving for America. All my friends, all the relatives, everybody was crying, and I was happy. I wasn't crying; I was like, "Man, I'm getting out of here. I'm going to go to the candy store and the toy store. I'm going to find money in the street. What's better than that?"

But then, I felt some emotion in Naples when my mother's brother came with his wife Lina to say goodbye. And then this big ship moved from the port, and everybody said goodbye as if you're going to another world, which we were. That's what America was, a different universe.

Inside the ship, it was a party; I loved that. There was drinking, there was this guy that was from the same town, he was older than me, and I was hanging around with him. And a few days later, my brother, my mother, and my father got seasick. They didn't leave their cabin. I was out every night and partying and enjoying myself and going to bed at two in the morning. The next day, I'd show up at the restaurant which was almost empty.

We had about three or four days of very bad weather, but then things calmed down. Eventually, we got to New York. We saw the Statue of Liberty. We were on the *Michelangelo's* deck, my parents were feeling better by then, and I told my father, "Come on, let's go look at the statue!"

And then I said, "See, dad, this is the Statue of Liberty. Now, you can't boss me around anymore. This is a free country!" And I started smoking in front of him, and the rest is the way my life began in the United States.

Four

The *Michelangelo* was coming into New York. It was a pretty great morning; it had just stopped raining, and it was cloudy and a little foggy. Approaching the Verrazano Bridge and seeing the Statue of Liberty, I remember even now feeling my heart beating a little bit faster. I knew I was entering a land of opportunity, a land that I thought was going to be like a candy store. And then, of course, in a very short time I learned I had to work hard to get what I wanted. I didn't mind. I was used to work. I'd make a fair living, and I'd be okay.

The *Michelangelo* docked around 10:30 in the morning, and they were unloading the holds and everybody's luggage. My uncle, my aunt, and my cousin, they'd come to pick us up and had driven all the way from the Bronx. Their house was in Morris Park, 1823 Hone Avenue. I'll never forget the address.

We lived there with my aunt, Josephine, and my uncle, Giuseppe Farruggio, same name as mine. They let us use their finished basement; there were a couple of bedrooms and a kitchen, it was all pretty private. They were very generous: they helped us, they paid for everything, and they fed us for a good three months.

If I think back to my first couple of days in U.S., it was really great, actually. I didn't miss my town in Sicily. I think the second day I was in America, I dressed up in my Italian suit, an English-style suit that I'd bought in Canicatti, complete with a tie and shoes.

I walked outside on Hone Avenue going towards Morris Park just to look around. At the corner, there were four or five young guys my age, and one of them asks in Italian, "Hey *guaglió,*" (that means 'Hey, young man') "Are you Italian?" I stopped and looked at myself, I was like, *why is that guy saying that?* So I approached them, and I said, "How do you know I'm Italian?" in Italian, of course. And one of the kids says, "Hey, dressed like that, you got to be Italian. We know what an Italian looks like." They were all Italians and immigrants like me.

We connected. I became very close with one of them, Alfredo; he was from Calabria, and his father had a pizza shop. Alfredo worked for his father making pizzas. Maybe a week, two weeks later, my brother got a job. This one guy came to America from my family's village, and he was working in the gold district on 42nd or 43rd Street. He told my brother, "Well, I'll get you a job there." So, my brother Vinny went to work in the city. And then, my uncle was working as a gardener in a cemetery. So, he took my father to the boss, and they gave him a job there. And my mother, after a little bit, she also found a job in a laundromat, where they washed industrial clothes from restaurants and hospitals. Three or four days later, I got my first job in a pizza shop on 204th Street in The Bronx.

My aunt had told me that a lot of Italians went into the pizza business. A guy would go and learn the business, and then he'd get his own shop and do very well. And I'd noticed early on that there were a lot of pizza stores, like every block had one, sometimes maybe two, so obviously it must be a good business.

Anyway, that pizza place where I got a job, that's where I learned my first important words in English: one, two, three. When the owner was teaching me, he was probably around 70, maybe more. I went to work for him, and the first day he says, "I'm going to teach you, when they ask you for one slice of pizza, they go *one* it means *uno.* Remember that. When they spit it and you hear *choo,* like they're sneezing, it means *two.*"

That's when I pretty much started serving behind the counter. I put my apron on for the first time in my life and went to clean the tables. It felt like it was somebody else that came from outside of me doing it, you know? I was really uncomfortable and shy. But then, soon, I got used to it. I recall it being a very strange time, because I was trying to find a job that would pay me the most, but at the same time, I had too many things to do. And then, I learned how to be a little less shy.

Yeah, that was my first job. The first day, my cousin took me to the job. The next day, they told me what bus to take and walked me to the bus stop.

I had to walk for about half a mile to the bus stop and take the bus. I was told the bus would stop running at Hone Avenue. I thought *stop* meant the bus stopped and didn't move anymore, you know, it's the end of the line. The bus stops, everybody gets out and then they go different directions. Instead, there was a bus *stop*! That means, it's one stop and then it keeps going. So, I waited until the last bus stop. It was maybe, two miles, three miles past my street. We didn't have cell phones; I didn't know how to use the regular phone. So, I walked back to Hone Avenue, hoping I was going in the right direction, until I found the house and my uncle. I tell him that, "The bus stopped over there!" He says, "No, no, actually, you should have got off at this stop." I didn't understand the word *stop;* it meant something else for me.

At the same time, they told me there was a night school for English. It was Columbus High School. I went there for adult school, even though I was not an adult; I was not even 17. I went to night school because during the day, I would do any kind of work that was available to have money.

I didn't stay in school long. Basically, I learned what I had learned in Italy when I went to accounting school and there was English as a second language. I learned, "What's your name?" "Where do you live?" Phrases like that. They taught me the same thing. But then, because of work, it wasn't easy to go to school every night.

My cousin Tony was remodeling bathrooms and doing tile and marble work. He took on me and my brother, Vinny, to work for him part-time for about a month, so we weren't working every day. We worked only when he needed us. I was also painting for somebody a couple of days a week and working at an auto body shop.

I went to work for Tony a little bit, but then, when he didn't have any work, I went back to the pizza shop. If there was another job opportunity that would pay, maybe 50 cents more per hour, I would try different jobs, but eventually, I'd go back to the pizza shop to work. That was the more available job and easy to get. It was hard work, but it paid well; you worked long hours, and you're making an okay salary. I remember getting $90 working 60 or more hours a week.

I found another job on Tremont Avenue, where I was an assistant pizza maker. I cleaned the tables, washed the dishes, and after about three months, the pizza man I was working with, he was in the bathroom, and a customer came in and ordered a pizza.

I didn't get the pizza guy out of the bathroom. I wanted to make a pizza. I'd watched him a lot, and I knew I could do it. I went ahead and made that pizza, and when he came out of the toilet and saw what I was doing, he said, "Wow, you did that? It's very, very good."

So, he started teaching me, to make me better. And in the next three months, I was making more pizzas every day and getting used to it; I was getting better and better.

Then I got a good job offer on 149th Street in Harlem. The place was pretty busy. I told the guy I was a pizza maker. To be honest, I was not a pizza maker, but I could do it if I worked slowly, a few pizzas at a time. But in this place, the guy expected me to be faster and also speak English better.

I was there for about three months, and one day he came and started yelling at me. He was just screaming! I said, "You know what? I don't want to work for you. Take your job and shove it," and I left.

So I found this other job in City Island, in a very slow place; we made maybe 20 pizzas a day, tops. I was by myself, and sometimes the boss would come in and help me make a few things, and then he would leave. That's when I met my first American love; this young, beautiful girl called Angela. She made my job more interesting, and it was an adventure.

When my father decided we should move to Brooklyn, I had to leave the job and the cutie. I was 17 years old; she was probably 15, a pretty brunette.

We moved to Brooklyn, and we were pretty comfortable. I don't know if we signed a six-month or one-year lease because I don't think we lasted one year. I was not paying attention to any of those things.

After we were in America for close to two years, we found this apartment on the second floor of a building. Some relatives, second cousins, owned the place, and we moved there. For my brother, it was easy. By then, he was working in the Diamond District in New York, making rings and jewelry.

My mom found another job in a laundromat, and I went to work with Angelo, a guy from Castrofilippo. It was in the East Village between Fourth and Fifth Streets and Second Avenue in Manhattan. I saw people sleeping standing up, I got held up two times at gun point. I mean, the Hell's Angels, the Los Angeles motorcycle gang, were our customers, and they were coming to our shop to eat. They had a house, and when we were going home at eleven o'clock at night, there was always loud music, girls, motorcycles, and noise. It was exciting. The Hell's Angels with their tattoos and gorgeous women! It was fun being there!

We parked next to where they lived. My boss took me home at night. I would take the train to go to work at two o'clock in the afternoon, and then we would close around 11, and he would drive me home. He lived in Brooklyn also. And that was pretty much my life. I would go home and watch a lot of TV and repeat everything the next day.

I did that for a couple of years. After a while, the owner of the pizza shop taught me what to do, and I learned other recipes to make pizza and sandwiches and some small dishes.

Lillo Carlino, who my family knew from Castrofilippo, had a pizza shop and he talked me into partnering with him in another pizza shop he wanted to buy.

I agreed. I think it required about $5,000 each to buy this place. So, I asked my father and my brother to put the $5,000 together, which they did, and we bought this pizzeria. The funny thing was, we thought this place was making a lot of money each week. We told the owner that we wanted to see in one week how much income his store was making.

The guy, he was not too honest, so he was sending in a lot of people; he was giving people money to come and buy pizza. So, we thought it was doing well, and we bought the place. And then, the next week, I think it was $1200 a week income in sales. And then the second week, we got like $600. Lillo and I, we looked at each other, and he asked, "What happened? Well, I guess he fooled us."

I started doing delivery; I started putting signs up; "We have specials," and within about a year, I took that place from making $600 a week to $3,000 a week in sales. Whatever I did, I did all by myself. But that's when I realized I was capable of making it work.

Then a few months later, I hired a helper.

Maybe a year later, an incident happened. I got into a fight with some high school kids. I was behind the counter, and they started bullying me. They were Sicilian-American, born in the States, and they thought they were in the Mafia. They were badder than me, in a way they thought they were more Sicilian than me, and they were grabbing pizza without paying. I was 5'4½, 120 pounds, pretty skinny. They were like football players and weightlifters, you know, they were built bigger. I'm not proud to say that one time, one of those kids grabbed the pizza and I said, "You can't do that!" And he said, "Shut up, guinea!" Guinea was a word the Irish called the Italians. It was very demeaning, and the Italian immigrants didn't like that word at all.

So he tells me, "Shut up, guinea, or I'll put you in the oven!" And I told him, "Come back here; come and put me in the oven!"

This stupid guy came around the counter and approached me and he got close to me, and I had a knife because I was making sandwiches, and I poked him. The knife went in about half-an-inch, maybe an inch, right next to his balls. When he saw that, he ran away.

I called my partner, Lillo; I got scared, and I was excited too! I really didn't notice that I had stabbed the kid, but I knew it when I saw blood on the knife! They left. They didn't call the police; I didn't call the police. I didn't know what to do. Me and my partner, we closed the place and went out to eat some Chinese food. He tried to calm me down, and the next day, I went to open the place, and at nighttime, about four or five cars came, full of guys with baseball bats. They destroyed the pizza place; they beat the shit out of me. One of the guys was punching me straight in my face, and at that moment I thought, *they're going to kill me*; I knew I was going to die. When he punched me, I just fell down like I was out. I think they got scared that they had killed me, and they left.

Me and Lillo, we sold the place after that. We got our money back because we had clients, and it was easy to sell it. The place was more in demand than before. That was a hell of an experience for me because I got to run the place all by myself. Even today, Lillo is still a good friend.

Then I went to work at Queen Pizza, which was great because they were making the best pizza. A lot of the places where I worked before, I didn't stay long because I didn't like the product or the owners. But in this place, it was really the best pizza. The owner was a perfectionist, and they kept the recipes secret. They had a special way of making the pizza dough. They knew other pizza guys would steal the recipe, and so, they had only the chef making the dough; they didn't show us. But it was a spectacular pizza dough, and today, I know what they were doing. I worked there for about a year, and I remember refining my skills.

The pizza crust was good, and that was pretty much the base of the pizza. Also, good tomato sauce, good quality stuff. And like I said, those days, I was not interested too much in what they were doing, what kind of product they were using, I was more interested in the technical part—the temperature and such, the actual manufacturing of the pizza. It was a great product, and people loved it more than any other place that I ever worked. So, that was another proof that if you make a good product, people will love and appreciate you.

I worked there for a year or so, and they paid me very well. When I started working as a dishwasher, I was making $90 a week, working 60 hours. At another job, I was paid $120, working 60 hours.

In the Village, I was making $215, and then I went to work at Queen Pizza for $250, working less hours. Shortly after that, I got a better offer to go work in Brighton Beach.

For a while we lived on Eighth Avenue and Forty-Fourth Street in the building owned by the second cousins. It was nice, a cute little apartment. Then, for some reason, the plumbing clogged up. It was a pain in the ass. Because I had long hair, I had a big Afro, and when the sink clogged, the second cousins blamed me. So we moved again, down the block on Fifty-First Street, above a pizzeria. This apartment was full of roaches. My God, I remember getting home at night, and I would turn on the light and the roaches would be running fast from all over the place!

I fell in love again, while we lived there, with this young girl from Castrofilippo, but it didn't last long.

Then I met Antoinette, the love of my life. I lost her because of my drinking.

Her family was from Calabria, and her uncle was a famous singer. She'd grown up in Paris, but now lived in Brooklyn. The famous uncle came to New York for a concert, and I bought a ticket and went to see him. She had told me, "If you go to the concert, don't say to my uncle that we see each other because my father doesn't know, and they don't want me to date anybody." So, I went to that concert, and I got drunk, I went to the uncle and said, "Hey, how're you doing?" I introduced myself like I'm a big shot. I said, "By the way, I know your niece, Antoinette. She's my girlfriend!"

The next day, I went to pick her up when she came out of school, she looked at me and she turned around and she never looked back. She didn't want to see me anymore. For a long time, I was devastated; she had left me, but I never really understood why until later…

I started working right away, but my friend Rosario was going to school. He met a couple of school mates, and he introduced me to them, and during weekends we used to hang together. We'd go see movies or go to the city on our days off. We'd see each other whenever we could. We were pretty young and innocent people, not street smart. There was this other guy, Mauro, from Padova, who came along. He was more of a city guy, so he was smoking marijuana at that time. He introduced marijuana to all of us around '73 or maybe '74. I was about 21 years old when I started smoking pot.

So, we would meet at night, different places, different clubs. I was the only one who had a car, a 1962 Mercury. Sometimes, I'd pick them up and then go clubbing and after that, I'd drop them off. Then, another friend came along, Vittorio, a guy from Milano, and he introduced us to skiing, so we started doing that.

I was working. All my friends, they did not have steady jobs. I had a job and making good money compared to them; double the amount they were making, maybe $300 a week. By the end of 1977, I was making around $400 a week in Brighton Beach. But I was working six days a week, you know, from 11 in the morning to 10 at night.

So we had this group; we'd go see Italian concerts, doing a lot of things together whenever we could.

I was still living with my parents, and we'd bought a two-family house. We were staying in one apartment, and we rented the other.

I loved the nightlife, the clubs. My friends, they started becoming hairdressers; two of them, actually. And they got in with the in-crowd; they were working in the city, they'd know what clubs were hot, what was an after-hour place to go; and they had friends that took us to those places. So, we'd finish work, not even shower sometimes, just change clothes in the car, and go party all night, and do the same thing the next day, you know, three or four nights a week.

I was not saving any money, but I wanted to start my own business. At that time, my boss, he drank beer all day when I was working for him, and his wife was more or less running the place. One day he told me, "Sooner or later, I'm going to retire, and I'm going to sell this place to you." And he kept me on a string, you know, and I worked there for about four or five years with the hope that he was going to sell me the place. But it was a lie. He never did, and I realized that I needed to move on.

Working with all those people, it was an educational experience. I saw how everybody did it, and I got my own opinion and decided I could do it, creating my own recipe and my own mix.

When I was working at Royal Pizza in Brighton Beach, I went in business with this Black customer. He talked me into buying a pound of marijuana with him; he told me he could sell it and double our money in a week. But then, he's smoking all the pot and giving me seeds and stems! I didn't get my money back. Another lesson learned.

The Russians started coming to Brighton Beach, and I learned how to drink vodka.

I remember that there was a conflict between the Puerto Ricans and the Russians. The Puerto Ricans felt like they'd been there for a long time and the Russians, they'd just arrived. The Russians were getting harassed, with Puerto Ricans yelling, "Fucking Russian, what're you doing here?" The Russians told me about it and said, "There's a bunch of Puerto Ricans out there. Every time that we pass by, they scream at us!" And I went with the Russians to say, "Let's go kick their asses," or something like that, maybe. But I don't think we ever did anything.

At Royal Pizza, it was pretty much the owners that would do the pizza dough and the sauce, and I was always in the front making pizza and dealing with the customers. My technique was getting faster. I wasn't able to handle a lot of orders, but I learned. It's just pretty much, like being a driver; the more you drive, the more you feel comfortable behind the wheel, and I was feeling more comfortable making pizza.

The owner was an older man, and I got a lot from him about what he learned from the older people. At the time, he was in his seventies, an Italian from Calabria. He was doing this for probably 30 years, and he taught me how the oven worked; taught me about what kind of flours that will be better and how much time the flour needs to be fermented before you make the pizza and how many hours will be best; and what the oven temperature should be. He taught me how to maintain a clean environment, and opening and closing. He shaped me, like in the army. And that was in 1976 or '77. I found that a lot of the customers that lived in New York and moved away came back to eat in one of those places. And they said, "Wow, I miss this pizza. This pizza is not the same pizza that I ate in Texas or Florida or in North Carolina. If you make this pizza over there, you'll do very well."

My friends and I were very involved with the Italian community. During those days, there were Italian concerts, there were Italian movies on Sunday. The Italian culture pretty much was there, in Brooklyn. And where we lived was an Italian neighborhood and it's like you didn't miss Italy in a way because a lot of immigrants from my village, they were living in the area, too, in Brooklyn. There was a lot of mixing with my own people. There were weddings, funerals, always something going on.

Italian singers used to come; we'd go to concerts. We would shop in the same Italian supermarket, butchers, bakeries, clothes stores, and we'd listen to the Italian radio station.

I didn't have any American friends, only the girls. We dated the American girls because the Italian girls, they were too strict, and the American girls, they were more available, let's put it that way.

You remember that movie? *Saturday Night Fever?* I lived on Eighth Avenue and Forty-Sixth Street. The movie was made on Sixty-Fourth Street and Eighth Avenue. So, I went to that club where the movie was made. I can tell you, the movie looked a lot better than the real thing.

I had the platform shoes and big heels with bell bottoms and the buttoned jeans or pants, tight shirt, gold chain and the crucifix. Those were the days in Brooklyn.

I remember when I went to watch it in the movie theater. We were passing joints like it was a party, like, everybody would be smoking, and inside the theater it was all foggy. We'd go to a lot of discotheques, there was the Boathouse, Infinity, Speakeasy, Monastery. And then at the end, Studio 54. Often, after work, my friends would come over to the pizzeria where I worked, and we'd cook; we'd be eating and drinking and playing cards all night. I always went home at about two or three in the morning and did it again the next day.

I was reckless with cars. I had a couple of accidents. I was driving drunk, and I had some pills. There was one accident, I was the third car, you know, and one car hit another car, and the other car hit another car, it was like three bumper cars.

I used to get into drag races. I had this Fiat 124 Coupe, six-cylinder, and one time, I challenged a Porsche. I said, "Let's race," and we were in Brighton Beach, and the Porsche driver says, "No, really, I don't want to race you." But he did.

I was with this girl in my car, and he was in his Porsche. So, we got on the Bell Parkway and going towards Kennedy Airport. And going 120 miles on a 50 miles-an-hour road. It felt like all the other cars, they were parked. The Porsche was going probably 150 miles an hour. I lost the race.

We never got stopped. One time I raced for $20, I was with my friend Antonio, and this kid with a sports car was next to us, and we raced from Sixtieth Street and Eighth Avenue to Eighteenth Avenue. It was like, 10 blocks, for $20. I stepped on the gas; I beat him to win $20.

I was getting tired of working at a pizza shop. Robert De Niro had made the movie *Taxi Driver*, so I changed jobs. I became a taxi driver for about six months. I was always in the city; a lot of clubbing, a lot of drinking and driving, and I thought it was cool that I would drink all night, then go get the taxi in the morning. I'd drive the taxi all day, then go to sleep and wake up at midnight, one o'clock in the morning, and go out. It was a wild time in my life.

The first passenger I picked up was an old lady in her 80s, she got in the taxi and told me, "Drop me off at this address." I probably made a wrong turn and she started screaming at me. She says, "Let me out! Let me out! You've going the wrong way!" She didn't even pay; it was about four dollars.

I'd pick up people I saw in the clubs, guys and girls. I would go around those places and know what time they'd leave. I was doing a fair business picking them up at seven or eight in the morning, from the after-hours clubs.

There's a lot of stories in Brooklyn: *Saturday Night Fever*, racing on Sixty-Fifth Street, throwing up on a policeman's shoes...

One time, I'm in a parking lot with my girl, and I turn around to see somebody watching us making out. I went after him with the car, and I wanted to kill him; I was serious. It was a time when I was losing it; I was out of control! There were a lot of drugs, a lot of drinking, you know. Me, I was more drinking than doing drugs. I was just starting to realize this maybe wasn't any good. So, I thought, if I get out of New York, it would be the right thing to do.

I began thinking New York was too much for me; I was getting burned out, I was drinking a lot and spending all the money I made. I didn't see much hope inside myself. America the candy store, the place I could do something, it was getting smaller. I decided to start looking for a job outside New York.

I worked for a lot of different people in New York, I mean, if I didn't like it, I would quit. If I were to like it, I would stay.

The men I worked for were doing a really good job, a really good business. I worked for other people, too, and some of them were ignorant, and they still succeeded!

So I'm asking myself, what's going on here? And then, I realized that if you work hard, and you do a good job, and you're serving a good product, you can succeed. You know, that was a really simple concept. I think if I learned something in New York, it's that.

Immigrants like me, they started their own businesses. After a few months of thinking, I had planted the seed; I needed to get out of New York, because if I didn't, I was going to get stuck there. I started looking in the Italian newspaper *Progresso* for job opportunities outside the city. I made some phone calls. I called a job in Texas, I called a job in Florida, I called a job in Virginia, and this man, Guy Henson, he asked me how much I wanted. I told him and he says, "How many pizzas can you make in an hour?" I said, "I can make as many as anybody in your shop."

He hired me on the spot, on the phone. I took the train from Brooklyn with my luggage, and I came to Union Station in Washington, D.C. He picked me up, and we get in the car, and he lights up a joint. I thought, "Shit! I'm running away from this, but here, it's catching up with me again."

I became his pizza guy. Anyway, we opened Guy's Pizza & Subs and it was very, very successful. I was the star behind the counter. At the back of my mind, the reason I wanted to get out of New York was to do something on my own, but I started with that job. I said to my boss at the time, "Listen, I think I'm the reason why we succeed here, and I would like to become your partner, fifty-fifty. You can open another store if you want, and I can run them with you. You can be the business guy." He didn't take me up on my offer. Instead, he says, "I'll sell you 25 percent."

I told him, "No, I want 50 percent, or I'm going to leave."

And I did. I called my brother Vinny who was in New York and said, "I found this place that I want to open, you want to come? We'll do it together."

At first, he wasn't sure. He said, "What are we going to do there? We don't have any money."

I had negotiated a deal with the owner of a place in Woodbridge, Virginia. I was working, but during the night, I'd go in my car with a six-pack of beer and explore the area. I would drive around and fantasize about where I wanted to put my pizza shop. And I was in Woodbridge one night and saw this cute little place, which had a lot of cars parked, but it was pretty much run down; there was no business. There were a lot of young people hanging around, not spending any money. So, I went inside, and I asked the guy behind the counter if he was the owner. He says, "I am."

I bluffed and I said, "I heard this place is for sale," and he says, "Yeah, it is. Who told you?"

I said, "Either it is or isn't for sale. Does it matter?"

We started talking and we negotiated $20,000 for the place. There was nothing I could use in a pizza shop. I gave the owner a $3200 deposit, with the promise to give him $400 a month for three-and-a-half years. The rent was $300 a month in 1978.

Vinny came later. Me and him, we painted, we did everything. I went to some used equipment place, I got them to give me credit, and I bought a pizza oven and a little dough mixer. We'd get lettuce and ham from the supermarket. I opened the place up in June for my birthday and started doing okay. Within three, four months, we were getting good income and good sales. My brother-in-law Fortunato came on board, too, as a partner, so now there were three of us.

We didn't have employees, just us. We cooked the sauce in the apartment that we rented up the block, because we didn't have a range hood in the restaurant. There was a stove in the apartment, and we cooked so much sauce that we destroyed the stove! When we moved out, we had to buy them a brand-new stove.

Three years later, I was burned out again with the lifestyle. I was still in contact with my friends in New York, and every other weekend, I would fly there and go party. You could drive into National Airport, park in the lot outside, lock the car, walk into the airport, and catch the Eastern shuttle and go to LaGuardia. My friends would pick me up, we would get the cocaine we needed—the guys already had a connection to buy some—and party Friday, Saturday, and Sunday. Monday morning, I'd fly back and be a pizza man in Virginia.

But if I think about it, I always say that every young man and woman should live in New York in their 20's for a couple years to learn what life is. New York makes you or eats you alive and spits you out. It's a tough city. A lot of people get stuck there because when you're in New York, you think the world ends at East River Drive and West River Drive, but actually, the world begins there.

But I was getting burned out with that life. It really was not too much fun. There was a discotheque next to the Woodbridge pizza shop. So that's what life was: pizza and drugs and disco.

Five

I learned something from everybody. When I came to Virginia, Guy Henson didn't know anything about the pizza business, and he hired me to do the pizza. And that was successful. After I left, he went out of business. That told me I had something in my hands that was worthwhile; it was a combination that was going to work. And then, really, really, I think, it's this country that makes you want to do more. After I opened the first Joe's Place in Woodbridge, it was the people; they saw that I had a good product and I had a good work ethic, and they said, "Oh, you should open another place."

I had already thought about that. It was just like in Brooklyn. They said, "Oh, if you were to open a place in a different state, you would do better because this product is good." It was a compliment to my know-how. They wished everybody could enjoy that product like they did.

And in my mind, I started thinking, "Well, in Woodbridge, it's a population of 30,000. If I were to open a place in Bailey's Crossroads, that's 200,000 people, I could do 10 times more business. The percentage is more people and more customers."

Woodbridge was the first experiment, because we, I say we, because it was my brother and my brother-in-law, and we were all pretty much one. We started getting customers. It was a small place, and I was inviting people from the discotheque.

We really exploded! I was able to make the location known in the area. I was able to make people aware that we existed. Plus, we had a good product, and that made us grow faster, and got the sales going up. One thing that we had going was, we were doing a lot of sandwiches, 10 to 20 dozen a day, and a lot of pizzas. And then, I put together this thing called the "Hippie Roll." I learned it in New York, and then I made it the way I liked.

It was Italian sausage, which was spicy or mild, with peppers and onions. But I'd cook the green peppers and the onions in a way that they'd come out really flavored. And then, I'd roll it up in the pizza crust and bake it. We'd sell them for 85 cents, then at the end, about $1, $1.25. We were selling like four or five hundred in a day.

But I was drinking a lot. We were really going strong, but because of my drinking situation, it knocked me out. My partners were not too happy, and I was not happy, and we ended up selling Woodbridge.

Next day I bought a ticket and went to Italy where I spent the summer. My family followed me to Sicily, and since I didn't want them to know how much I was drinking, I went back to the States. I found a new location in Bailey's Crossroads and negotiated a five-year lease, with four five-year options. My brother Vinny came, and we opened the new Joe's in February 1982.

We were modernizing with new equipment and had a lot of success. We invited my brother Lillo and his family to come from Sicily, and we would make him a partner in the next restaurant.

Lillo came, and we opened the third place in Arlington. By that time, I had realized that when you open a restaurant, the important thing is to negotiate the lease, and more important than that, it's to have an option to buy the real estate where you do business. And the way I will do that is, we will negotiate the price—how much on lease and get an option to buy the building within five years. And the first two places, I did them with the price already decided.

I said, "Within five years, I will buy this property at this price," and they agreed.

I had two options: owner financing or the bank. But I started learning about negotiation and deals when I first did the Arlington restaurant. I found that in Arlington, there was a chain of pizzeria called Godfather's Pizza. They came in from the West Coast and opened a bunch of places around here, but they didn't do well. So, two or three years later, they started closing. They had negotiated great leases with landlords. I knew a particular place was available; I liked the location, and I called the company and asked, "You guys are going to close that location?"

They said, "Yeah, actually, we are."

I said, "Well, I'd like to buy your lease," because they had over 20 years paying $3,800 a month but the price didn't go up for 15, 20 years, or it went up very minimally.

So basically, it was a better deal than the one I had in Bailey's, because in Bailey's, it was twice as much. It was a place they'd built two years before. So, I offered the Godfather company enough for the lease. They left everything in the store: the oven, the register, the kitchen equipment, the furniture, and I used a lot of it.

So I like to say that I gave the Godfather an offer they could not refuse. They didn't even blink. They said, "Okay, send him a lease." I reviewed it and sent them a check, and we had a deal. And I think, we made an agreement with payments I had to make within a short period. But at that time, we had some money, enough to do that. That was in 1985.

I didn't have an option to buy it, so we ended up buying the property because I called the landlord almost every month, three, four, or five times a year to say, "I'd really like to buy your property," and he said, "The property is in a family trust." For years they said it wasn't for sale, but I said, "Please, if it goes for sale, I want to buy it."

And finally, one day he called me and said, "We're ready to sell." He quoted me a very high price. But we negotiated it to an agreement. We had the bank finance it with a small business loan because it was already owned and operated by us. We had our own business, and the bank was able to finance it easily. That property now, it probably has doubled or more in value.

That's when I started learning what the market was doing, and the big boys, what they did. I thought, "Shit, how did they get a lease?"

What I learned was that a big company goes to a landlord and says, "We got it here. We are a rich company, if you work with us, you're going to stay there forever and make money. If you rent it to somebody else, they're going to go out of business!"

But the truth is, big chains go out of business, too; there's nothing secure about it. Anyway, we opened the Arlington store, and the rest is history.

And after Arlington, I did the Vienna restaurant. I opened the store in 1991 with a nice, fair rent, whatever the market demanded. The landlord sold me the property, and I assumed a note, because I didn't go to the bank, and then, I think, in 10 years, I paid for the building. The same money it was costing me for rent, it was costing me for the mortgage, even less actually. The mortgage didn't go up, but the rent would go up if I didn't buy it. So that piece of real estate, I bought it for $950,000, and now, it's worth about four million. If the landlord had not given me the option to buy it, now, I would have nothing. We opened the place, I think, in '91, and did really well for about 10, 15 years. And then, after 2018, it wasn't doing well, so we closed it.

Fairfax City was another deal by ourselves because it was a really big space, a lot of parking, and a good location downtown. The same deal was going on there, about 20 years of lease at an under-market price. I ended up buying that lease, that was about

$125,000, something like that. But that was with a note with no option to buy the real estate. The only reason I did it was because the lease was very low and very long. With that property, I got lucky. After I got settled, I called my landlord every year and said, "I want to buy this property. Sell it to me." There was a MacDonald's near where I had my place. The landlord said, "I can't sell you just Joe's; you have to buy Joe's and the McDonald's. It's one parcel."

I didn't have any money, but I thought I'd figure something out one way or another. I was going to make it happen.

Finally, one day, the owner called me, "I'm going to put the property on the market. I have a buyer, and he wants to buy it for $2.2 million." I said, "I'll buy it for that price!"

He said, "If it doesn't go through with the other guy, I'll call you." Well, it didn't go through, and he called me, and I called my brothers and my brother-in-law; I told them we had this opportunity, and I had a meeting with them. And it was chaos; they thought I was crazy. That was in 1999, I would buy a property for $2 million. They said, "What if something goes wrong?"

I walked out of the meeting. As I got in my car, the landlord called me to say the people that were trying to buy before had come back and he was going to sell it to them, since he already had a written offer from them.

I said, "Mr. Smith, don't worry about it. If it does not work out, I'll still be interested!"

About one or two months later, he called me. "It's yours if you want it".

And guess what I did? I didn't have any money, but I had the lease of the restaurant, which still had many years left. I originally had 20 years, and I'd used about seven. That lease was less than $4,000 a month. So what I thought was, well, I have 13 years of lease, maybe with $35,000 of savings each year. That's about

$455,000 that this lease is worth to anybody that wants to buy this property. So if I were to tell my landlord I didn't want to buy and he had somebody else to buy it, they'd have to buy me out and I could ask for at least $800,000. And probably, the buyer would give it to me.

I called my brother, Lillo, the one I thought might be interested. I asked him, "Do you have $350,000? If you do, I'll sell you 30 percent of this deal and your down payment will make us buy it. And I will put up the lease for collateral."

He said okay, and we made the deal. We bought the property, me and my brother. I was 70 percent, and he was going to be 30 percent.

So now I still had the pizzeria with McDonald's next door paying the rent because we had to buy both lots. I mean, McDonald's was paying very little. The property was cheap, basically because of the lease. Both parties didn't pay too much rent. So, we were making about $7,000 a month in rent from MacDonald's and from Joe's and there was a note for almost $2 million. We were paying over six percent on it, which made the note higher than the rent. We became partners for the land, not for the restaurants. And it was good.

One year later, I get a phone call from a broker; they want to buy the property. I told them it wasn't for sale. They say, "We'll offer you $6 million." I tell them, "Yeah, it's still not for sale."

I really was not planning to sell it. I called my broker, who says, "I think it's a good price, but I can get you more." So I sold the property, and that got me to understand a lot more about how real estate worked.

Before all this was going on, after I opened the Joe's in Fairfax, I had to hire a friend, with the idea that he would help me open a bunch of Joe's. And he helped me a lot. I thought I was going to teach him what he was going to do. He worked in Arlington for about six months, then when I opened the Fairfax store, he managed it. We opened that one, then we opened in Gaithersburg. In Gaithersburg, I worked out the same deal. There was already a restaurant on the property, and I told the owner that I would rent it, but I wanted an option to buy with a fixed price.

From 1998 to 2003 when we bought it, real estate in Northern Virginia and the D.C. area skyrocketed; it tripled. We had an agreement that the rent was $10 per foot; within those five years, the rent was $20 or $25 per foot.

So in Gaithersburg I was paying the rent; I was paying $10,000 a month. That was high, I gave the owner what he wanted for rent, but he had to give me the option to buy it for a fixed price.

He figured I wasn't going to buy it, so he'd collect the rent for nearly five years, and then I'd be out of business and wouldn't buy the property. But I did very well there for five years. Then, the fifth year, I said to him, "I want to buy your building." He couldn't say no because we already had an agreement.

We went to closing. Before the closing, the lawyer ran a title search. It turned out the seller, he'd bought the land and built the building, and we found out the next-door neighbor claimed one foot of the building was on his property.

When I went for closing, my title company and the bank said they couldn't finance a building that was on somebody else's property.

And then, I went to the seller, and he said, "You don't have to buy it if you don't want to."

I said, "No, I'm buying the fucking thing. You're selling the building for this price."

We went to litigation; at the same time, we contacted the neighbors and they agreed to allow us to keep the building permanently for a small fee. If for some reason, we wanted to redevelop it, they'd get it back. But as long as I kept this building, I could stay there for life. We worked that out with the next-door neighbor. We went to court, and we won. The building owner had to sell it. He appealed, and we won again. He ended up selling us the building. And during all that, I stopped paying the rent. So, the last year, he didn't get any rent income, and he had to sell the building for the price that we agreed. That property now is worth three times more.

At this point, I learned so much about commercial real estate that I realized there's more money in real estate than in pizza. I could sell pizza and buy real estate. And I realized, wow, these are what the big boys are doing. Really, I'd never make that kind of money in pizza. I made a living, I made a very good living in pizza, but I never got millions, you know?

So anyway, going back to Fairfax, we sold it for a spectacular price, and we purchased three buildings and put around a million in each building.

I bought property in Gaithersburg, Maryland, two buildings, and another building from one company that sold it to me and my nephew and my brother's company.

So, I bought the property that I used to pay $925,000 for and two other pieces of real estate. And because there was a loan on the property, we cleared quite a lot of money. I took some money, my nephew took some money, my brother took some money.

So now, my real estate is growing. We have three new places that are away from the whole group, but I only have my brother as a partner. In Arlington, we were three partners; in Vienna we were four; and then in Fairfax, I was by myself until I got my brother to help me with the financing, and he became my partner, too. So, right there, we have three pieces of real estate financially growing a significant amount in the last 20 years. All that gave me a lot of education in wheeling and dealing in real estate.

In 2000, I went through my divorce, which was an emotional disaster and forced me to regroup because I was in no shape to run a new business. Six months before my divorce, I had bought a property in Waldorf for $625,000. It was a Friendly's ice cream place, and then I changed it to JoJo's Pizza and Buffet. I opened it and then closed it pretty quickly, and a year later switched to Mamma Maria's New York Pizza.

Mamma Maria was the same concept as Joe's Place. But because it was a very long distance from where I had other places, and the driving time to get there, I wasn't able to make it work. There was another lesson for me. I had a family friend, and we had an agreement that he was going to work there. His father was a chef, my friend was going to be a manager, and I told him, "I will give you 25 percent of the profit. And then if everything works out well, I'll give you 25 percent ownership of the restaurant."

Mamma Maria started very well, we were doing really good, but then the gentleman who was supposed to be the manager, he started flirting with a waitress, and the other waitresses were complaining.

I told him he had to stop that, or I'd have to get rid of him. I said to him I didn't want that kind of behavior there. He denied it, but the other people at the restaurant kept telling me it was still going on.

So then I told his father, who was the chef. I said, "If he doesn't stop doing that, I will have to fire him."

His father says, "If he leaves, I leave, too."

I said, "You know what? Both of you leave." They did, and I shut the place down. And that was another stupid thing I did because that could have been a goldmine.

That place was closed for about a year, and then I leased it to a car dealer. He spent a lot of money on the property. He was there for about two or three years, and then the economy went bad around 2005. He was a luxury car dealer, and he gave me back the key. He said, "I can't pay rent anymore."

The property was closed for a couple of years until I rented it again. I learned that if you give time to real estate, it'll cure itself even if you make a mistake. So, that was from making pizza to real estate. That was a big transition that I had to learn. I didn't learn by choice; I learned because I had to survive.

By then, the only Joe's that still existed were in Vienna and Arlington. But in 2018, we closed Vienna. By this time, Joe's was running a buffet, and COVID shut us down in August 2020.

The worst difficulty I had during this time was that I was a partner, and I had my family working with me. I wanted them to see the business the way I was seeing it versus just running the customers and the business. The business was easy because people loved what we did, they loved the product, they loved the restaurant. We had a great price, great product, and the business was booming. But the issues there were in-house. There were a lot of disagreements with the way I was doing things. That sort of pulled me away from wanting to do more stuff with family.

Six

When I got married the first time, I was 33. I went back to Italy in 1980 and I met my future wife, Mariolina. I didn't know her, even though she came from my village. When I left in the 1970s, she was only five years old.

She was from my street; we lived five doors apart. So, when I got back, I noticed her. She was a young, beautiful girl. But I didn't think much of it, you know, and those days, I used to come back every few years. Eventually, I noticed her again, and I started something with her. It was interesting. I was 25, and I let her notice that I was interested, but nothing happened. Until 1984, when I was still interested in her and trying to approach her, but she would always tell me she had a boyfriend.

When I went back in 1985, she was in her 20s, and she didn't have a boyfriend, I knew that. So I did it the old classic away, I called my sister and asked if she could do me a favor and talk to Mariolina and tell her I liked her.

I asked my sister, "Can you do that for me?" And she said, okay, fine, and she went to Mariolina's house and told her that, "My brother is interested in you, but I know that you had a boyfriend before, and he wants to make sure if you're interested, so he can approach you. He doesn't want to be rejected; he doesn't want to disturb you for any reason."

Mariolina said, "No, I don't have a boyfriend, and I'm interested too."

When we met, I expressed that I was attracted to her now, and I would like to continue a relationship. At that time, she had left the village and gone to Rome to work.

She said, "Well, I'm going to go back to Rome in a few days, but I'll come back, and we'll get engaged and we'll see what we're going to do."

I didn't talk to her parents. I worked everything out with her. She went back to Rome, and I visited her there a couple of times. About a month later, she came back to the village, and we started to get to know each other. I didn't know how this was going to go, but I was pretty open about it.

She told me she didn't want to start a relationship if I had to go back to the States; she didn't want to be in a long-distance relationship. She said, "If we get married, I come with you." I agreed to that, so, we got married December 4, 1986. But now, honestly, I've moved on.

She'd never been to the United States before, but she had relatives—aunts, cousins—that lived in New York. We came here, and we went and had a nice honeymoon in Italy; we went to Rome, Florence, did a few things, and then we flew to the States. We went to the Cayman Islands where it rained a lot, so we left and came back to the U.S., and then we went to Canada, because she had a sister there. We flew there, and on our way back, the immigration stopped her saying, "You can't get into the States."

I said, "What do you mean? She has a visa!"

But her visa was for a one-time entry, and we'd already entered and left.

The next day, I went to the American Embassy. They didn't pay attention to me; they said, "No, you have to fill out an application, blah, blah, blah."

The second night, I rented a car and we made sure that we got to the immigration roadblock around two in the morning, and she pretended she was sleeping. I showed my green card to the officer, and he went around the car and said, "Open the trunk."

I opened the trunk. My wife is pretending to sleep, and they let us through. We went to Buffalo, and left the rented car there, and got a plane ticket, and flew to Washington.

From then on, we didn't leave the country until she got all the papers together. And then, we got married in a Virginia court, we got a lawyer and got all the documents together, and eventually she became an American citizen.

If I think back, when I was in Italy, when she was still my fiancée, it was really the best time of our relationship. After we got married, I think the energy changed. When she came here, we were not connected the way we were connected for the first four months. And for some reason, we were growing apart, not together, and I was thinking that we weren't going to make it; it wasn't really comfortable. Then, she got pregnant with our first child, Roberto, and I guess that kid pulled us together in a way. I was accepting all that was going on. And then, we got the second boy, Enrico, and our marriage got shaky, around seven years.

We had the third son, Alessandro, and I thought things were pretty okay. I planned to work hard, run the business.

When I got married, I had two restaurants. By 2000, when we got divorced, I had five restaurants and a lot of stuff on my plate. I was busy, but I always made time for my kids. I'd stop by their school, went to soccer games, but by 2000 the marriage was over. The major thing in the divorce, she said, was that I didn't pay attention to her. She said I was always working.

It wasn't an easy divorce; it was a really shocking divorce; it really knocked me out for a couple years. It took me about five years to get over it. Now I don't talk to her, but we got three kids that we made. I won't say we have a great relationship, but we are the parents of our kids.

By the time I got divorced, we were doing okay with the business. I was always investing all the money we were making at the restaurant. I wasn't making a lot.

I started closing some of the restaurants. The good thing was I had owned the real estate, so it was easy to close it and get another restaurant to pay the rent.

Mariolina was never involved in the restaurant. She didn't know what I was doing. She was very disconnected from my business world, working at Benetton as a salesperson. Just something to keep herself busy, making enough money to buy clothes for herself. We had a house; she took care of it and would cook and keep the kids fed, keep the house in order.

During the divorce time, it was really difficult for me. I wasn't paying attention.

JoJo's was a whole-day pizza, pasta, and salad bar buffet. We were doing very well when we opened it, but during the divorce, about a month later, it just got run into the ground. I closed the one in Gaithersburg, then I closed the Fairfax one, and then there were only three restaurants left. My brother, Vinny, was running one in Bailey's; my brother, Lillo, was running one in Arlington; and one other in Vienna was run by my brother-in-law. That freed me up. Thank God they were handling them.

I started running marathons all over the world, I ran 16 marathons from about 2002 to now. It was a distraction. I was taking care of myself running, and traveling, and doing my own thing.

Running was probably one of the best things I have ever done.

I started when I was 49 years old, at the beginning of my divorce. I was about 187 pounds, and now I'm down to 160.

The truth is, I was numb. I was pretty much on automatic, running five Joe's Place with my brothers. I was always working or taking the kids to game and events, and getting more involved with the family, with business, and with my 12-step program. I suppose I was on a plateau.

When my divorce started occurring, it was like I was hit with a two-by-four. At that time, my ex-wife had registered me at a gym. She said, "Well, I think you should join, it would be good for you…" So I started going to the gym. There was the frustration of the divorce, which was causing me a lot of pain. I ended up going to the gym pretty much every day, and then I started running.

I was running a mile or two, and then I realized I could run three or four miles without thinking of my frustrations and my stress. I did not really want to be a divorced man; I did not want this to happen. I kept running, and I did that for a while. I was burning a few pounds.

The first marathon I ran was that fall in Chicago. I went to Italy, and there was a friend of mine, Pino, who had run a bunch of marathons. I told him I wanted to run. And he said, "Well, let's run together."

We ran the hills of Castrofilippo together. Those hills are 500 meters above sea level, and it was so beautiful there! While we were running there, we met another friend, Angelo. We started talking, asking "what's up," and we decided, unanimously, to run the Chicago Marathon in 2002.

I didn't know if I was really going to do it, but I committed. I was 49 years old. I remember we trained so hard, a lot of work, I think it was in October.

Now, 20 years later, the three of us will run again in Chicago.

I came back to the States, and my friends came about a week or so before the marathon. I met them in New York, and we went to the wedding of Angelo's cousin.

The next day, we got in the car, and we're driving to Chicago; we're going to do this marathon. We created T-shirts that read, "Three Runners from Sicily."

We checked in at the hotel, and showed up at the starting point, and we started running. And that was probably one of the most spectacular achievements that I thought I could do with my body. It was unbelievable, running a marathon!

We finished it, which was amazing! We celebrated by going to the best steak house in Chicago. We ate, and we enjoyed ourselves, and we toured Chicago before and after the marathon. We shot thousands and thousands of pictures when pictures cost a lot of money.

And then later, we just looked at each other and said, "We'll do it again!" And we did! We registered to do a marathon in Paris in April.

We drove back to Washington, D.C., and those were the days when a sniper was killing people there. We were actually scared because we were driving from Chicago to Washington, and we listened to the news of the sniper who was now in the Virginia area.

After three or four days, my friends Pino and Angelo went back to Sicily, and we all started running and training. In April, I flew to Paris to run the marathon there.

We met, the three of us, and Angelo and Pino had brought their wives—both of them were named Mariella. We spent some time doing the tourist thing.

That was another spectacular marathon. It was really cold, and we did the same thing: we showed up at the starting line, and we started running with everybody, and I knew I was going to finish it—that was pretty much the goal, to finish it.

The first marathon, I did it in four hours and 47 minutes. In Paris, I think we did it four hours and 23 minutes. Of course, we said, "Okay, we're going to do it again." So we did New York. After New York, we did Venice, Florence, Rome a few times, Berlin, and Athens. In the States, I did the Marine Corps Marathon and the International Marathon in Washington, D.C., and Phoenix, Arizona.

For the first five years, after my divorce, the marathon was my companion, my support. I wasn't capable of working. Luckily, my brothers and my family understood. They knew about the divorce and let me do my thing.

I'm still running. I still want to be the oldest marathon runner in New York city. I'm 69 now, so if I keep running, I'll probably be one of the oldest ones. I don't know how old I'm going to be; probably close to 100, so I have to look up who the oldest marathon runner is, and I have to beat him or her.

Today, I'm running an average of three times a week, about five miles at a time. During the winter, I'm in Florida, and I run or walk four or five miles every day.

I'm keeping my weight and my sanity. I think running has been a really big part of my life. Probably, if I have to rate things from one to five, maybe the second most important thing in my life is running. Stopping drinking is the first one, running is the second one, and becoming a father and developing my business are a few others. Running and being sober saved my life.

Seven

In 1981, when I sold the first Joe's Place, I was making pizza and subs in Woodbridge, and it wasn't just my decision to sell, it was a decision made by my partners, my brother, and my brother-in-law. It was a decision made in desperation. They couldn't handle me because at that time, I was addicted to drugs and alcohol.

I had some DWIs, seven of them, I think. I knew I had to do something about it, but I didn't know what. I had no concept of anything that could be done. I had a motorcycle because I was trying to escape the police. I had the DWIs, and I thought the police would not recognize me. I'd ride the bike from Woodbridge to Bailey's in the wintertime wearing a ski suit. Actually, one time, the police stopped me, and my driver's license had been suspended, and they asked me, "License?"

I thought he was asking for my automobile license. I said, "Officer, I don't have a motorcycle license."

The policeman said, "You'd better get one."

He didn't ask for an auto license, and if he would've asked me, I would have told him I don't have that, either. But he only asked me for the motorcycle license. The next day, I sold the motorcycle to my sandwich guy.

I really liked cars, though.

In New York, the first car I bought, for $50, was a 1962 Mercury.

I thought I had arrived! And then, me and my brother, we bought a Mercury sedan, and then a Firebird. When I came here, I bought a Chevrolet Impala, and I sold that to a friend who never paid me for it. He got into an accident, and two weeks later he collected insurance that I had been paying, and he kept the money.

And then I bought a 1970 Porsche, a two-seater. When I opened the Joe's Place at Woodbridge, I had the Porsche, but then I got rid of it and bought a four-cylinder turbocharged Mustang. After that, it was an Italian sportscar, a Lancia Zagato. I was still drinking then. When I stopped drinking, I bought a Mercedes 380 SEC. I didn't have a driver's license, it was still suspended, and I wanted the police to think I was conservative, you know?

It worked until I got stopped once; there was a street checkpoint. They said, "Driver's license."

I didn't have it. They gave me a summons, and I ended up serving three nights in jail at the Fairfax County Detention Center. At that time, I was not drinking, and I realized the time I spent in there while I was drinking, this was a completely different experience. I knew I would never go back there again.

I eventually got my driver's license, and I never got arrested anymore.

So back in Bailey's Crossroads, this club opened right next to my restaurant.

Some people from the club, they came to eat in the restaurant, and one of the guys, he had an Italian last name, he noticed that I was always sitting down at a table and drinking beer. He approached me and said, "Have you thought about not drinking? I see you're drinking all the time."

I told him, "Not really." Because I really didn't see any other option except for drinking.

He said, "Well, if you want to stop, I'm a part of this 12-step program that can help you".

I said yes because I didn't know how to say no. So, I went to that meeting. It was at 5:30, September 11, 1982, and I've never had a drink since. From that moment on, my life changed.

I got married four years after that. My first wife did not know me when I was drinking.

I'm really grateful that I chose that path. And today, it's been 40 years since that choice was made. If I hadn't gone into the program, I don't think I'd be here. That's how much the drinking and drugging affected me. I would probably be dead. I was drinking and driving, I was reckless, my life was out of control. And I don't think I would have lasted another 10 or 15 years. Coming to the program, that was my chance to do the right thing, but, you know, it doesn't mean when you do the right thing, everything works out the way you want.

That's when I went to Italy and met Mariolina and fell in love. I'd been in the 12-step program for four years. And I was ready to assume the responsibility of being a husband and a father.

Eight

I have sons, three of them; they are men now. They used to be boys, and now they're three men. Roberto was January '88, and Enrico was December '89. It's like 22 months difference. And then, Alessandro was June '94. All of them have different personalities. They're three completely different human beings. And you know, there's no single approach; three different boys, so, learning a lot how to do, what to do. I'm proud of what they're doing. Roberto is finally graduating, you know, he left art school about five years ago without completing. He's a very good artist, photographer, and musician.

He had an accident when he was 16. It was during the summer in Sicily, and he broke his leg. It was a big battle to get him healed. And then, he got back on painkillers; marijuana was helping him. It was pretty much overwhelming. He got sick, he had some issues with himself, and now he's doing a lot better. He finished school; he's really trying hard. He's pretty happy.

Then, there's Enrico, the second one. There was a lot of jealousy between the first born and the second born. And then the third one came along about five years after Enrico.

So, Enrico is a very loving kid. He's probably the most loving kid in the world I know. He got addicted to drugs, but he's doing good now. He's been clean for about eight years, and he's getting his life together. He's about to become a drug and alcohol counselor. He's starting a new life.

The normal routine was he would come to me every other weekend, and I had him through the whole summer; I took him to Italy. So, yeah, it was some rough times for me. Now he's quite himself and just trying to do alright; he's a good man.

And then, there's Alessandro. He's another one, completely different. He always was the mediator of the three boys. He will go with one or the other, and they will deal with it. He will move them, in a way. He was always a pretty clear kid, and he knew exactly what was right or wrong, so that he could be a judge, because he always took the right side. Maybe he learned from his brothers.

The other two, Enrico and Roberto, they started in Montessori; Roberto, until ninth grade, Enrico until sixth grade. He did preschool, and he started first grade and went to elementary school.

Roberto, he did elementary school in Montessori and went to junior high there. Alessandro went straight to preschool. All three of them went to McLean High School. Enrico did not finish. He went for home schooling; that was when he wasn't doing so well. Alessandro, he did good with school alone, he had the same friends since he grew up. But then, Enrico had different friends. He didn't have a steady group.

Each one presented a different joy and a different challenge.

Enrico had a learning disability. He had this situation, and we didn't know how to cope with it. We were trying to reach out to the school, but he was not cooperating. But you know, they were all good kids. They played sports: Roberto played soccer, then Enrico started playing basketball. Roberto's challenge began after he had the motorbike accident where he broke his leg. He was 16. That took a long time to fix. His knees are still not bending right.

I saw them every other week, so I didn't know, I wasn't there every day. I didn't know what was going on at their mom's house, but when they were with me, they'd have fun for the weekend because I would take them out to movies and do things with them. So, it was a fun time when I had them; we would do something exciting all the time.

Alessandro went to high school, then to Virginia Tech with a double major in business and accounting. He finished school *cum laude* at the top of the class.

And then, he went to work for Deloitte, which is a big international accounting company. After one year, he said, "Dad, I got to get out of this. I want to come and work with you."

I said, "No, stay another year. Learn the business more. You have a free learning opportunity in the company rather than coming to work for me."

He said, "No, I can't stay here any longer." So, he came to work for me. Now, he's been working at the restaurant for three years.

Alessandro was the only one of the boys who came to work in the summers. For the past two years when he was an adult, he worked as a waiter. Before that, he worked as a kitchen helper, which the other two boys didn't do. I didn't force him. It wasn't that I thought I was giving him an easier life because I worked since I was younger, so I would really push him. But Alessandro, he actually wanted to work. He liked to earn his own money. So, he is now the General Manager at il Canale and managing his own team. He's handling the finance and all the numbers. He's doing a good job.

I don't know if he is going to be the one who's going to follow in my footsteps. There's nothing sure. I would like to see that because I've been blessed to be able to create what I did with the business and the real estate, and I would like to see him take over the well-being of his brothers, so that they'll be able to know everything I was able to do, and it will stay in the family. I have a trust, it's a living trust, and he's one of the trustees. He will help other members of my family with whatever they want. My goal is whatever was created in my generation will go in the trust for education and medical emergencies. We will take care of the family to come, the family in the future.

I have two citizenships now: American and Italian. I think the one thing was because my kids are American and I want us to travel together, so me and their mother became regular citizens.

And another reason why I wanted to become an American citizen was that, before you had to say, "I am no longer Italian. Now, I want to be American." And I couldn't do that. I couldn't do that. I said, "You know what, I'm Italian and I'm proud to be Italian." I could not give it up. They changed the rules so you could keep your birth citizenship. And also, as I became older, I wanted to vote. And I could not complain if I didn't vote.

Nine

I started this concept called 90 Second Pizza four years ago in July, but it was in my head for about 10 years. I shared it with the manager who was working for me and he's like, "Let's do it. I'll do it with you." Because he was younger, he had energy, I decided to do it.

Ninety seconds is the cooking time of the pizza. You know, you walk in, it's no cash, you order and put it on your credit card. It's been doing really well. The first year we had it open, we kept it going, building a record month to month, every day. We actually broke even in 2018 and 2019. We had programmed it to do 30 percent more, but we did it by the same amount because of COVID. And in 2021, we are where we want to be. So anyway, the concept and the numbers and the structure, it's really a winner, and I want to develop more.

Right now, I think franchising is what's in the future. I'd like to do two more stores this year, to see if multi locations will work. Basically, in my experience, you must have two or three stores to be able to see how you can stabilize control in the system. So, I am opening two stores this year. Doing it with the right boys, getting my employees involved with profit-sharing and letting them be investors so they can have a piece of the action. It's a new idea that I want to try out—simply pizza and a bottle of soda, of water—not even a soda fountain. In the next location, I want to try salads and desserts.

Naples is where pizza came from originally, a couple hundred years ago. Pizza was made in the kitchen in Naples and stayed within Naples for probably 100 years; it was just a local food. And it was in Naples until early 19th century, and it started coming out of that city and started going to other major cities in Italy. And then, as of the last 30 years, it's been coming out of Italy and going worldwide. Now it's in Russia, Japan, a lot of other countries because it's a gift of Italy; it's something like the Coliseum.

There are some principles you have to follow to protect its integrity. You have to respect the guidelines. It's a pizza, it's tender and juicy, and it's made from double zero flour. Eight to nine hundred degrees temperature in the oven. It really cooks fast, and it comes tender, not crispy, and that's the classic difference.

Pizza is the food most eaten in the world. You can't mess up pizza, really. And pizza's good, and then it's excellent; and everybody knows good is the enemy of excellent.

I've been making pizza since 1970, that's what I've done. Gone to excellent. I think in all these years, I've learned a lot. I used to make New York style pizza. There's New York style, there's Chicago style, there's California style, there's Argentinian pizzas. Pizza is in every country; they make them with their own characteristic.

So, pizza, it pretty much satisfies all the cultures. Because it's flour, sauce, and cheese, originally. Then, they put other things. So, I did a New York pizza for 35 years. I discovered Neapolitan pizza in a way, like somebody has been driving a Chevrolet or Pontiac and then, they drive a Ferrari. I think that's the difference between those two products. They're both good cars, Pontiacs or Chevrolets, and there's nothing wrong with a Ferrari. It's about taste, and it's about the ability, usually, to prepare the pizza because everything is important. I mean everything we use, from the flours and the salt, it's important too. The tomatoes are important; mozzarella is important; it gives the authenticity, and you can tell.

An average person can tell the difference if you taste with an open mind. If you go with Neapolitan pizza and you expect it to have the same taste as what you've been eating from America, you're going to get blown out of the water, either negative or positive. Because that pizza is so soft and juicy. And so, I fell in love with the pizza the first time I tried it in Naples, and I fell in love with the Buffalo mozzarella.

You know, my original goal with Joe's Place was to go to other states. We were in Maryland and Virginia. I really wanted to take the restaurant to other states when I was younger, but it didn't happen for many reasons.

I opened il Canale in Georgetown, in D.C., and it became a tourist place. Politicians and singers and musicians and actors started coming and that made it more well-known. I won't be trying to repeat it somewhere else. It would be a nightmare.

The Georgetown location was right, and the product was, too. The city was ready for it, and it worked. The 90 Second is something you can put in college, business, residential, anywhere there's people.

I am considering it in Florida, but it could be anywhere, anywhere in the world. So, we'll see what's going to come out of that. I'm 69 years old. I'm not looking for a job, but I'm looking to lead this thing to the dimension that it will shape other people, maybe one of my sons.

I have one of my chefs who worked with me for five years, and now he's back and working with me again. He will make my product even better because he's a Neapolitan pizza maker. I'm a Sicilian pizza man and I learned in America, but he grew up in Naples. I learned a lot from him, and he learned a lot from me, and we're going to see if we can make this thing happen.

I am very satisfied today after COVID, we surpassed the capacity before COVID started. People want to come, but they're scared.

But the 90 Second Pizza is doing good. It's gone back to the way it was the year before.

I think the restaurant business, you're manufacturing the product, so you're buying the flours, tomatoes, onions…and you're buying that stuff wholesale and raw, and the customer leaves with a pizza in the box. So, you are manufacturing, and that takes one concept. But if you're retailing by being in a restaurant, then you got to have customer service in uniform, the right colors. And then there's the dining room, delivery, carry-out, your catering, it becomes complex. If you don't have the experience to keep it together, it dissolves. I know the best chefs. They get investors, they open their restaurant, they explode—they're doing excellent.

Six months later, nobody goes there. That is because the chef tries to become an entrepreneur, and he doesn't know how to be an entrepreneur. He knows how to be a good chef. He changes hats or he changes position, and he actually does not replace himself. You know, he changed position, but that position needs to be filled with people that want to meet your standards. You could be at the front and do the other part of the business and socialize. But if you move, and your assistants don't have the same thing you have, then it's just not going to work.

The people, the managers or the chefs, they'd bring their bad habits with them. You know, we have a cook or chef or dishwasher or a waiter, they come to your place, and they want to do what they know how to do. And then you have to say, "Okay, there's a vision!" My vision was to open a business, open a little pizza shop. And I didn't know how I'd always get it to work. We started creating the logo, and then we designed the uniform with the colors you use all the time.

And then, in my case, my customers demanded more of me. It was like, "Why don't you do this?" I have pizza and subs. "Why don't you make lasagna?" or "Why don't you open another place over there?" I'm like, "Why?" And, you know, they got me thinking.

So, I did open another place over there, because pretty much in America, if you're doing a good job, people reward you. In America, you give a hand, and you receive the whole body. That's been my experience. What I've done is add a product, and I was able to provide it with the best quality I could for the best price that I could to an average person.

The people liked it, and they did that over and over again, for years, for decades. You know, I started 1978, and in 2022, it's 44 years that I've been in business. A lot of growth happened, and I learned from a lot of mistakes, trying and failing.

But I think mistakes are needed in any business. It's a good thing that I've never had to make those mistakes again. COVID forced me to close the last Joe's Place, which had a good run for the money. But the concept was getting outdated, and I found that, eventually, it couldn't work anymore.

Now I am bringing Neapolitan pizza which is VPN-certified (Verace Pizza Neapolitan) to our customers.

Ten

Concepts are everything. They got me to where I am now. I started by making pizza in New York. I worked for a lot of people. And then after starting my own business, the way I opened my first store, it followed a concept that I created. There was nothing original, but it was something under my name, Joe's Place Pizza and Subs. We had about 10 different subs and many topping and pizza. And then I invented this thing called a "Hippie Roll." I created it because of my experience in New York. I made my own, in a way, my own thing. And that thing exploded! People loved it, and we were selling hundreds and thousands in a week, and that was in a little tiny place.

When I opened the restaurant in Bailey's in 1982, I still wanted to create an even better concept. So, I wanted it to look like a fast-food pizza shop. I am not going to use Pizza and Sub again; it became Joe's Place Pizza and Pasta because my concept involved pasta.

In Arlington, we started the concept with the waiter service. For lunch, we had to cook from scratch. Like, if somebody ordered pasta, or if somebody ordered sandwiches, we'd need to do that fast. We had complaints from people who had an hour, half-an-hour for lunch, and they could not wait. So, that's when I came up with the buffet. So, then it became Joe's Place Pizza, Pasta, and Lunch Buffet. The lunch buffet exploded. It was really famous. So we had Bailey's and Arlington.

It must have been 1983 or '84, the delivery concept came along.

At that time, a friend came and said, "You know, this Domino's Pizza, they deliver pizza in 30 minutes."

I'm like, "They must be crazy. It's impossible."

He said, "I'll show you."

So, we ordered a pizza from Domino's. It came in twenty-five minutes; I was timing it! So I applied for a job at Domino's, as a delivery driver, I went through their own training. When I finished the training, I started delivery from my Bailey's restaurant. It was really, really good in the beginning, but as the years went by, the large chains sort of took over delivery, and it was hard to penetrate it as a small business. I realized I was not going to be able to penetrate it. When I opened a store, like Bailey's and Arlington, delivery was okay. In Vienna, I never managed to break through.

In 2000, I created another concept, JoJo's. It was nothing original. There was the chain called Cici's which had only buffet. What I did, I made it better. I did a buffet with the pizza and salad and pasta. I took my buffet concept from Joe's, and I just made it all-day buffet. That was a concept that I should have really developed. But then, my divorce happened, and with all the stress, I couldn't follow through. I had to shut it down. It was successful for about a month.

When I was done with that, I looked at my background; I was able to evolve, to see what the market needed, and what I thought was just coming up. I think that was something that helped me to get here, because if I had stopped with the pizza and subs in Woodbridge, yes, I would have probably done well, but I wouldn't have evolved. And I think that's what happens to a lot of people in my business.

I worked with people in the '70s who I knew made a spectacular product, but maybe they're still working for other people, or they've started their own place, they keep doing the same thing. They open up a restaurant, a pizza shop, and they just stay there doing exactly the same thing over and over again.

I look at what the other businesses are doing to see how I can apply it to my business and be able to experiment with that.

I was able to take Joe's to five locations and wish I could have been bigger, but that was my capacity. My divorce pretty much sapped a lot of my energy.

I didn't get involved in my company for about 10 years. I was escaping and doing marathons and taking care of myself. And then, I got involved as a silent partner with an original Neapolitan concept. Then I invested in the idea. We took that concept to America, and I thought it was a lot better system than Joe's.

Joe's was a New York style pizza. It didn't have the originality or authenticity of a product born in Naples. That was created many, many years ago, in the 1800s, I think.

So the idea is to be able to do that product now just the way it was done then. It was like a breath of fresh air in Washington; it was really fresh and unique. There was not much going on in D.C. 10 years ago, only a couple of places were doing it, and we were able to execute it better, and it went well.

We started with Joe's, something very simple and not original, which was the standard pizza shop with a couple of subs, and we kept adding to it and taking away the stuff that didn't work well. Adding and taking away. And often what I love, it's not even on the menu.

After you write a menu, every two or three months you have to evaluate it, and I would take out the stuff that didn't sell to put in something new. And just keep on recycling every three or four months, look at it again. If something sells only one or two a day, you don't want it on the menu. You want something that sells 20 a day; you concentrate on that. It will make your operation faster, fresher, and the fresh product moves. But if people are not familiar with the food and not buying it, it means that something's not right.

The 90 Second Pizza is supposed to be the best pizza you can do in the fastest way. I'm thinking about going to an A-plus location, really the best location. I need about 1,000 to 1,200 square feet. Right now, I can get that for probably $80 a foot. I don't want to build from scratch because that would take six to eight months. I want to get a location that maybe was a place that closed; a coffee shop or little sandwich shop or some other business that shut down and where almost everything would be already built.

Then all I have to do is put my equipment in. I got a mixer, an oven, and a pizza table, and computer system. If everything is already in place, I will be able to do it within three or six months.

I'd like to stay pizzeria. I almost always want to change something, maybe to put in an espresso bar with muffins for breakfast. And then I think it through: You've got to open it early in the morning...I think it's complicating things; you confuse the clarity of the concept. You want to be known for making the best pizza or for making the best muffin? And the end, the way it gets to people, I think it should be the best pizza. That's what I want to be known for.

Yes, maybe a good wine. It goes with pizza. Maybe a good salad. Maybe, there's also pasta. But I don't want to be like the grocery store.

Believe me, I've been tempted many times. Right now, instead of all pizza, I'd like to do 33 percent pizza, 30 percent restaurant and 30 percent beer and wine and dessert. So, which one do I want to massage the most? It depends. Sometimes when you have some employees and a chef, they work with you, but they want to change you, they have new ideas. I've always been tempted, but in the end, I believed that I want to stay with pizzerias.

I am a pizza man. My goal in this book is to be able to inspire somebody to see that if you believe, and when you sell it, people like it, they're going to come back. So just keep on doing it. Eventually, the lid will come off, and the dream will come true. You'll be where you thought you weren't going to be or where you're never going to be, but eventually you'll be there.

You wake up, and you look around you, and that's what's happened to me. I look around, I'm like, "Geez." I mean, because I really concentrated on building the concept, building another restaurant, or building a real estate portfolio, building a bigger house and another house. It's like, sometimes, I look at my life and I think I'm a builder. Anytime I wanted a house, I thought I bought it to live there forever. And I remodeled it. I cleaned it. But then, the fact is, I didn't live there more than five to seven years.

So, I'm like a doer machine sometimes. If I see something, I look at it, and I see what can I do to make it better, or what's wrong? Why is it dirty? Why does it need to be painted? Or, it's still fine; let us make it shine. So, it's always, I want to build it to improve.

When I walk in the restaurant, I just go by scanning, and I pick up what's wrong. And that's not good. I don't like it because I get irritated when I see it. But even if it was 95 percent right, and I see that something is on the floor or something is dirty or something's not in the right place, it bothers me.

Over the years, I had to learn not to let it disturb me so much. I'm the kind of person that goes to work next to the pizza guy, and I'm always wanting to improve him. My guys have been doing it for five, ten, fifteen years, but I always see a better way and a faster way to make a product. I know the way I want it to come out and get to the customer's mouth. I want the customer to taste the whole product, not the sauce, or not the bread only, not the cheese only, there should be enough of everything, so it becomes one, one flavor.

If I work with the pizza guy, or even if I work next to the cook, it's the same thing, it has to be balanced. I have to make sure that the pasta is cooked the right way. Because you can buy the best pasta in the world and then you mess it up while you are cooking it. Or you put too much salt or too little salt, too much sauce or too little sauce. It is so simple; it's about winning or losing. It really is. Because if you don't have that kind of supervision, or you buy the best Romaine lettuce and then you cut it and then you use it 24 hours later, and it's rusty. For me, that stuff, it's like cancer. It is poison. And I've been fighting all the time to really prevent that in all the areas and in all the restaurants.

The dishwasher, same thing. You have a washing machine, and you have the chemicals, and you have a good man working. Sometimes, some of the people that work, they've never seen a commercial dishwasher machine. And if you don't check the chemical before you start your shift, or clean the filters that clog up, you are washing dishes and glasses and they don't come clean. And they get to the table dirty because really, it's a link from the dishwasher. The other employees, they don't even look at the dishes one by one, they just put them out in bulk, and it becomes automatic. And by the end of the day, the customer gets a dirty glass, a dirty dish because of your habits.

You have the dishwasher, you have the machine, you have the chemical, you can do everything right, but then if the person is not trained right, the problem works against you. All the time, if you're able to execute right, it works for you. If you don't execute right, it works against you. So, either you get customers, or you lose customers. Really. You put positive energy or negative energy.

Same thing for the tables and the floor. I walk around my restaurant; if I see a little piece of paper, I pick it up. And you know why I do that? To set an example. If my employees see me pick it up, they'll pick it up too. If I step on it, they'll step on it. It's leading by example.

The bathroom is another thing…the door handle…I go to a restaurant, and I grab the door and I see it's all greasy, I don't go back. I really don't because I noticed that they don't see that greasy door handle or those greasy bathrooms. How are they going to see what's in the refrigerator or what they put in my food?

It really doesn't cost any more money to make a good product or a bad product. It cost the same, because you're still paying the rent, the light, you're buying the product, and then you mess up the execution! Why does that happen? Why do people mess it up? Because they don't have any experience in the market and the restaurant business.

Everybody wants to go into the restaurant business. They think, "Oh yes, I know how to cook. I should own a restaurant." But in the restaurant, you produce and you retail at the same time. You might know how to retail it, but if you don't know how to produce it, it's not going to work.

People come to me and say, "Joe, I want to open a restaurant." I usually say, "Save your money. What do you know about restaurants?"

They say, "Well, I know how to cook. And when I was little, I used to wash the dishes, and my mother or grandmother has a lot of good recipes."

So I ask, "What kind of restaurant do you want to open?" They say, "Well, I like to open a place that has this good wine and nice uniforms. And this art on the wall, and…"

Then I ask, "Does that concept you're trying to do already exist?"

They say, "Yes, there're a couple places like that. They're doing it over there."

I suggest, "Why don't you go there and get a job. You know, for minimum wage, and see what they do. Train yourself for free and see if you like it, see if you're capable, see if it's something real."

I usually like to discourage people unless they already work in restaurants. Even the great chefs fail in restaurants, even a great manager fails, because they think they can make a restaurant successful simply because they are a good chef or because they are good managers. The manager doesn't know the back of the house, and the chef doesn't know the front.

It's a lot to digest, but for me, it's natural. It's my life, though I'm learning not to take it so seriously now. I took it really serious for many, many years. Now I go into the restaurant, and I compliment my employees, but I don't correct them. When I have something, I only talk to the managers. I don't really talk to the rest of the employees anymore. Because I don't want them to think if you talk to them, especially to the assistant cooks or the busboys, if you say something, they might believe I'm accusing them of doing something wrong. They take it very heavy because they see me as the owner, so, if I would say "No, do it like *this*," they get their feelings hurt because they think, "What? I'm doing it wrong?"

So I talk only with the management about things, and it has been a lot better for me because when I see something I don't like, I can go to the manager now. I trained them to do it the way I'd do it, the way I want to do it. And it's working really well because they hold me to a high standard. Now, my managers correct the problems.

The manager and chef, they are pretty much at the same level, so they talk as equals. The communication gets even better that way. It's been really a big learning thing for me. I think I'll eventually get it right.

In the past I micromanaged because I had to control all the departments. Now a manager says, "No, I got it. I got it." So, when I understand that he's got it, I let go. And that's when the transformation happens; I have to step up to my own position being the CEO and do a CEO job versus micromanagement. It was damaging. It was keeping me from growing. And it didn't release me from the stress.

Eleven

The other reality I want to discuss is real estate. I wish I had known the structure of leasing a property with the option to buy it. Let's say, I had five Joe's restaurants and that I would have leased all of them in shopping centers. Number one, it would have been hard for me to get out when I had to get out because I had leases tied to my name. In the '80s, in 1985, I started noticing that I was creating something, I had to buy the real estate. But I had no money to buy it.

What did I do? Every time I signed a lease, I would say, "I would like to have the option to buy the property and a lease for 25 years." I structured these leases to have renewable options every five years. I have the option to stay or go after five years and have the option to buy the property the first five years. So, I would say in the first five years, if I'm doing really well, I would tell the owner, "I'd like to exercise my option to buy the property, and you have to sell it to me. We can either get an appraiser, or we can say now what the price is."

On some of the leases, I had a selling price we'd agreed on earlier when I signed the lease. On others, we either agreed with the owners on a price, and for some of them, we had to get an appraiser. But I bought all the property for which I had the option. And five years later, 10 years later, 20 years later when I started closing the stores, I owned the properties.

On some, I put a "For Rent" sign, and somebody else rents it, and I lease it to them. That way, I was not tied up. And also, the real estate, the last 20, 30 years, it's increased a lot in value, so I really made more money in real estate than I made in pizza. Just to say that, yes, I sell pizza, but I bought real estate at the same time. I was making a fair living and I was building a real estate portfolio over the years.

So, that was another winning strategy that I think helped me a lot. Because now I find myself with five, six pieces of excellent commercial real estate worth a lot more than what I paid for them originally.

I've had many failures, but I consider all my failures to be a great lesson in business. And I think in real estate, time will cure any real estate mistake I made. Well, maybe if you buy it somewhere else in the country, it takes a lot more time. In this area, close to Washington, D.C., you might make a mistake paying too much, or something that goes wrong, but in two or three years, it regulates itself.

But yes, I did make mistakes. You can call them mistakes, or you can call them situations, things that happened when you play the game. Anything in life that you really do, there's always a risk. And the reward for doing nothing is you stand on the sideline; you don't get anything; you're looking at everybody else smile.

I had a couple of times when I bought a piece of real estate and leased it out after I closed Joe's. I got tenants in, and then they stopped paying rent because they were not doing any business. I had to hire lawyers to get them out and find other tenants. The new tenant needed me to put in money to help them. I put money in, maybe $50,000, to help them get started. That means you buy real estate for three years, and you lose money one way or the other. That was a lesson I learned: the real estate game is a real expensive game.

Then I bought another property. It was an excellent location, but my lawyer did not see something in the title that said I could not rent the property to a place that was competing with the one next door.

And here I am. I bought this piece of real estate for $2 million, and within two months we're getting a chain that wants to rent it from us with a really great lease. I think it was like $200,000 a year in rent. And then they realize they can't compete with the business next door. So six or eight months later, they back out of the lease, and then it took them another two years to rent the property. So, I carried the empty property for another two years.

That happens sometimes. I learned in the real estate business that you also need to be selective with your tenants and try to know who they are, their name, and that they can do what they say to pay the rent. Now I get involved personally. We meet them, realize who they are as humans, and we know their capacity and what they've been doing.

Now, all our properties are leased, but still every property has its own ups and downs. The last one was in Vienna, and it was closed for three years. Now, we have two tenants, one downstairs and one upstairs. And the property, if I want to sell it, I could sell it for four times more what I paid for it 20 years ago,

Another concept was, we're going to try to go towards organic. I told my general manager, we've got to go towards organic, and we went there. It helps expand my business, and we're really working for our customers, working for our product. Also, I think I'm working for my employees, just like my employees are working for me. All the unsalaried employees get bonuses. So, when they're cutting onions, if they take off an extra layer, they're actually losing a few pennies for themselves.

The waiters and the bosses, if they do a good job, they know there's a good product behind them, they can do better tips, so they make money too. I have all of them involved to help me raise the bar. And then when the bar gets raised, everybody makes a better living.

This happened by experience, by testing. I had a different system before that would reward only the chef, and the manager, and GM. But I found out they get spoiled because they were making too much money. Everybody under them, they were making less money, so the chefs, and the managers, and the GM become like kings because they're making so much, and they control the other people.

Take the dishwashers. You can get a dishwasher every day coming to apply at your restaurant. Every day! But I don't want one every day, I want one that is going to keep the job and teach him to really do a job the best way.

I think in the last three, four, five years, my people are staying because some of them, they hear what another employee tells them. "I used to wash dishes, now I'm doing preparation." They see they can improve.

One time, I ordered my chef, "You used to be a dishwasher, and you were responsible for the dishes and dishwashing machines. So, because you are now a chef, it doesn't mean you don't deal with dishwashing anymore. It's your responsibility. You have to help other people, when they come in as they are doing now, you have to teach them how you became a chef. You got to help them to do their job, lead them to success, so they can assist you in different ways."

The only thing is, often with the dishwasher and people at that level, there's a lot of low self-esteem, because they think it's the only job they could do, because there's not too much risk there. So, they think they're not smart, but it's not true. There's some great smart guys out there, they just have a low self-esteem, so they do the cheaper job.

In Italy, you know, you'd be an apprentice for 20 years, until the guy above you dies or retires, and then, you become the master. But you work for the family, or you buy the business.

One time we were in Sicily with a friend, me and an American guy. We went to the shipper to get some fresh Ricotta cheese, and the shipper was making the Ricotta, which is basically what is left over after you've made other cheeses. My American friend says, "Ask him how long he's been doing this." And the guy answers, "Well, I've been doing it for 20 years. I'm learning how to make a cheese." He was making the Ricotta for 20 years, and now, he was going to graduate to making the actual cheese! Even to me, that was a shock. In America, it doesn't happen.

The mistake is, you've got a kid coming out of college, and the people hiring want workers that have the experience. And that's the core model I try to avoid, because I want my people to come from the bottom up.

I don't have an established system for them to climb the ladder. Let's say, the chef sees somebody who is interested in learning and doing more, so he lets him, because it's really benefiting everybody when you got people coming in from the bottom up. It's benefiting the chef because, he sees somebody that could do a good job, and so he could trust him. He picks the people that can help him because he wants to produce the best product.

If you have somebody that is good, and the GM spots him, he'll let him move up. When they move up, they move up in salary, they move up with a bonus.

At the end of the quarter, we decide bonuses. The GM talks to the pizza guy, the head chef, and says, "How's everybody? Is everybody following the procedure? And blah, blah, blah… The chefs give him feedback. And my GM also evaluates the staff, including the chefs, and me being the owner, I have a fixed percentage of the quarterly profits for bonuses.

All the people in the kitchen are under the GM. And the kitchen head guys, they do it for the others. They give feedback. At the end, it's pretty much the GM who decides if he wants my opinion. And sometimes I give him my opinion if it is necessary.

But sometimes, I'm not in the restaurant. I might be going to Florida now, and maybe I'm telling myself that I want to come back every couple of weeks, for a day or two. Maybe I will, maybe I won't, maybe I won't come back for a month or two months. And I trust that my system is working through the numbers that I get to see.

The people at every level have got to be comfortable in their jobs. They can't be fearful, or they can't be threatened by other people coming up. The GM or the other managers would hopefully spot that.

My concept provides that my managers spend time in the kitchen, too. On weekends, we have four managers. So usually, one guy goes in the back of the house, and one stays in the front. We're watching the whole system all the time, through their eyes. Shall I say they do a good job? Yes! Enough so that I am comfortable even if I am not present. The truth is, I have the best team working for me.

So picking a GM and not a regular manager is a big job, because for me, the GM has to know everything about my operation; he has to learn all the systems, everything from the dishwashing to buying the food.

They don't do it themselves, but they are the ones that work with other people who do everything. So, if there's a problem, I go to him. And if he doesn't know, he learns about it, so next time, it gets done. It's all that process of learning. My GM now, he's been with me a year-and-a-half. The one before him, he was with me four years. And another one before him, he was with me for five years.

The GMs usually come from recommendations. I know a lot of people in the restaurant business, and a lot of people have worked for me in the past that I still have great relations with. I ask, "Do you know anybody?" I hire a human being manager, not somebody that I'll look at the resumé and say, "Oh, he's good!" The last manager, not this one, the one before, I asked a friend of mine that had worked for me for five years.

He called me and said, "I have this guy, he's a potential GM, if you need him."

I told him, "Well, I don't need a GM right now, but I can use him as a waiter if he wants to come on." So, he came with the idea that he was going to be a waiter for a while.

But you have to know that not everyone can be a good GM. At the time, the GM that I had, our relationship was not good anymore. He wasn't listening to me and actually rejecting my opinions. He was believing *I* should listen to *him*, so I had a conflict with him. He left the restaurant, and then he came back. He was my friend before he worked for me, so I had him back, but I knew the relationship was done. I didn't want to fire him; I was giving him a chance. But he was actually getting worse after he came back.

He'd show up late; he'd take more time off; he would close early; he would shut down the reservations; sometimes he would get someone else to open the restaurant or close it, so it got less people. He wouldn't do anything to make the business grow because he thought it was big enough. He says, "We're doing good. Why do you want to do better?"

When I expanded il Canale to take over the space next door, he was against it. And he argued with me until its opening. He said, "You shouldn't have done this."

I told him, "I'm glad I did it."

He thought I should open another store. I said, "No, I don't plan to open another restaurant. Another store is another lease, another manager, another pizza man, another GM, another this, another that. Here, we're going to double or triple the numbers without going to another store."

He had his own weird kind of conflict going on all the time. Like I said, the problem when people get to know me personally, I'm soft sometimes, and I give them the permission to be straight with me, to tell me what they think. And sometimes, they think my being a nice guy means I'm weak.

They think they can control the situation, but they forget that I'm the owner; they think they've become indispensable. That's the worst thing: when my employees start thinking that they're doing everything. When they start thinking that way, it works against the business. They start getting sour, and it's time to get rid of them because that's very negative.

It's like a kid; it's like family. You have people working for you because of the money, and that's another negative. I don't want people to work for me only for the money. I want people to work for me because they want to, and I want them to have their heart in the right place.

So anyway, that's when I made the mistake of hiring that GM. But then, I had proof that he was stealing, but I didn't tell him that because he was a friend. My accountant, my other manager showed me. The month he was suspended, there was no money missing.

And then, when he started again, he started to steal and when I got proof, I told him, "We can't work together anymore; I got to let you go." No explanation, nothing. He actually sued me a year later; he sued me because he said that I fired him because he was old, and I hired somebody young which was not true. And then, God took him, he passed away, and the case got dismissed.

I learned a lot. Because I had to move up from a mom-and-pop store to a corporate operation. When you start making the numbers I made, and I have between 40 to 50 employees, I can't run it by myself. It helped me to realize this, that I could be more behind the scene than in the middle of the scene.

I'm working harder now than when I first started. This is emotional work; it's not physical. I miss the days when on a Friday night I used to make 100, 200 pizzas! Now, it's all about public relations, it's political because you've got to be politically correct.

It's really a lot of juggling. You got to juggle your products, you want to make sure your place is clean, make sure the product is good, make sure the bills are getting paid, and all that. And then, you've got to make sure that nobody sues you.

It's a joke. It depends on what state you live in; Virginia and D.C. are different. But depending on where you are, there's more chances to get sued.

Before I went to D.C., I never needed a lawyer to do anything; it was more like normal, you know, starting a business and doing business. In D.C., everything you do, you need a lawyer. You have a sign; you get an inspector. You've got to show up early, and you've got to get your attorney, too. And it'll be time consuming with a lot of people who have nothing to do except hassle you. That took me away from doing the everyday things I used to do in Virginia.

I think I have to trust more, my team, my employees. Before, I could replace any employee on the spot when I chose. Now, I can't replace anybody, really. I can't work the oven; it's a wood-burning pizza oven. There are a lot of things, and because I haven't been doing it, I can't do it. So, I have to think twice before I talk. I think I depend on my people more than ever before. Now, I'm pretty much dependent on the system. And of course, when you get more than one store or restaurant, it gets way more complicated.

Going from one to two stores, it's probably the most difficult thing, because all the rules change. You're one store, you have to hang on all the time. Now, with two stores, you have two people doing the same thing, but you're not able to copy exactly the same way. With the second store, for example, the menu isn't going to be exactly the same, and you can't keep up with the changes. You have one less soda, or one less item on the menu, or one less wine; you're doing things differently in one store than in the other. You use the same product, the same vendors. And now, you're operating in two places; you have two places to watch. You've got to be faster; you've got to be more on the ball.

When you go from one restaurant to two, you weaken your first store because you're going to move some people to the other restaurant. These are the people you depend on, and now, you move them.

The new people, you've got to train them because they are coming in with their own habits. You've got to change mentality. It's not you alone anymore; now, it's other people and you've got to watch them.

Let's say, you have the computer system moved from one store to another store, and you make an exception, like, somebody wants the pizza served upside down, for example. And you do that request in the store, and then, that customer goes to the other store and asks them for the upside-down pizza, and they say, "We don't do it."

"What do you mean you don't do it? They do it at the other store!"

The world changes. It's like going from the first floor, the view from there is different from the view on the second floor, even though you're in the same house.

And when you do the third store, you have two places to choose from. So, maybe you choose one different item to put in the third store. If you're successful with two stores, the third store would be a little easier.

I paid my own dues. I started when I was 25, and I sold the first store when I was 28. And I reopened the second store when I was less than 29 years old. I had two stores when I was about 32, and three stores when I was 36. That was when I was getting married, I was going to become a father, and we were juggling the family. There's a lot that I don't remember; there was a lot going on.

Today it's different. Now, I can make any choice that I want. I realized why I pulled away from my family business 20 years ago, because it was harder for me to run my family with the disagreements we had. The customer was easy; I provided a good product, but my brothers and my brother-in-law, we disagreed all the time on the way I wanted to run the business, and the way they wanted to run it. I'd make some choices that created conflicts with them all the time. And that was a lot of stuff that was really disturbing; it wasn't making it easy for me.

I did a commercial that wasn't so expensive to make but was very successful. The commercial cost maybe $5,000 to make, and it was so effective that the buffet business was growing like five percent a month. We were all over the cable TV in Virginia and Maryland. We had five stores at that time and spending about $5,000 a month in advertisement with those cable TV ads.

We were growing like crazy; I mean, we were doing 200, 300 buffets a day at each store; we had lines. And I was like, man, I got the right combination with the TV! But then I'd go into the stores and some of my partners would say, "Stop spending all this money for advertising. Look how many customers we have!"

They'd tell me, "We're doing a good job; we don't need to advertise!" But the reason we had so many visits and customers was because I was advertising. And then, I'd go into another store, and they'd complain, "Why are we spending $5,000 a month?"

I heard that stuff all the time until I got sick of it, and I pulled the plug on the ads, and Joe's Place never hit those plateaus again.

Their own excuses were, the economy, people don't want to spend any money. They were telling me what I already knew.

Three or four years later, I convinced them to do another commercial, which would cost me $100,000. It didn't work. And they said, "You see?" I mean, that commercial was forced, it didn't have the right energy.

Oh, man, the things that I did to sell my products, I mean, every time I would open a store, I'd print 100,000 flyers, and I'd get four people hanging out at the 7-11, put them in my car, pay them $20 an hour, and put out flyers in a three miles radius, rain or sunshine, for six months at a time. To do 100,000 houses one at a time, it takes a lot. I did this in Bailey's, I did this in Arlington, I did it in Vienna, Fairfax City, and Gaithersburg. But my partners didn't know I did that. They thought the customers just came. The bell rang, the phone rang, and they were making pizza and that was because of the flyers.

One time in Bailey's, I put a big sign on the roof giving away $5,000 cash. That was like, 1983, '84.

For about six to eight months, everybody that came in got a number. We had about 10,000 participants! Anytime you eat, you get a number, you get a chance. The day of the drawing, we did so much sales, because an extra thousand people were buying soda, coffee, sandwich, pizza, waiting for the draw.

A dentist won it. He got the check for $5,000, and he became my dentist.

A lot of people, mostly young, say that one of the reasons I've been successful is because a long time ago, when I got started, it was easy to start in business, and now it's harder.

That's not true. It's a lie. I think a lot of the culture during the last probably 30 years has been cultivated to make people dependent on the government, or to make them dependent on salary with a lot of help from the government.

People don't have the necessity that we had before. Before, you didn't have a lot of the government assistance, so if you had to succeed, you had to succeed with what you had. I think as human beings, we have everything we need to succeed without help.

A lot of the time, I could say, well, people see the way my business is today, but they didn't see it when I started it 42 years ago with a few thousand dollars. I borrowed some money from family and friends, and I negotiated a deal with another small businessperson who was not making it. I was able to control my first location by promising, basically, to make it work. Because every time I start a business, I don't start because I think *maybe* it's going to work. I always start a business because I think it *will* work, and because I'm coming from a place where I have all *I* need to make it work.

The new generation, it's entitled. They think somebody else is going to do it for them, and the only thing that they have to do is manage the success. But the success, you have to build it from scratch. There's no social thing that will help you if you feel you are entitled. I think entitlement is the disease of the new generation.

And also—I don't want to get political about it—I think what changed from the past is that now there are more regulations, and those regulations, they were made by our government.

So, that's what I wanted to say, that it wasn't easier. No, it was hard back then, and if you believe it was easier, you'd better not get into the business world, because the business world is tough. It's hard work, and you're constantly worrying and making sure all the mechanisms move in the right directions. If something is out of tune or off the beat, it's going to slow you down and you're going to go broke.

Today, my focus is on always improving my model, always improving the way business gets done, because competition will always be there, and it was always there. Competition is not something that came just now. If anything, it's harder than before.

So, I am a witness that hard work, consistency, and trying to sell yourself is the key to success. My days are so full of stuff that I want to do. I'm like a kid in a candy store. I want to do everything. I've been to a lot of places in the world, and I will continue to travel. It gives me satisfaction, it gives me excitement, and it keeps me sharp. I don't do puzzles; I don't do typing. I don't take notes by writing. I don't read. I have an eighth-grade education. I don't really ever want to read a lot. I read what I need, but it's like I force myself when I have to read.

But you can't think every day is business as usual. Every day isn't equal; how can it be equal? I am constantly learning; it's like running a marathon. How do you become a better runner in the restaurant business? You're all the time trying to improve it, just like you are trying to improve the running, you're trying to take it to the limit.

For me, my running, it's a bit of a challenge, and it's a recreation. Probably, it's my stubbornness, you know, I can do it, I can finish it, and I finished them all even if some of them I walked at the end.

In business, you've got to be patient. I look at my latest restaurant here in Arlington, and it's not doing what I want. So I am there as often as I can be to coach my manager and chef. I've been leading from the back, and some things started moving, started getting a little bit better.

Twelve

Before I stopped drinking, I had this desire for entrepreneurship. I started the business while I was still drinking; I knew how to sell my product, I was always promoting the business, which was Joe's Place Pizza and Subs in Woodbridge. But I was powerless. Now, I say what I do, and I do what I say. Before, I'd say but I didn't do. It's been the difference between day and night with my entrepreneurial desire and with my showing up.

You show up and do the job. I have to give a hundred percent. If I had not stopped drinking, I would not be here. Because I had this mental confusion. I was not doing what I was thinking in my brain; I was doing things separately. I had my experience, my know-how to be able to channel what was needed in the right directions and be able to control it, be able to be a boss, a manager, a brother, a father, be able to be all those things I wasn't before. So, everything I knew, I might have learned it, but I didn't know how to apply it. When I stopped drinking, I was able to apply them. That's pretty much it.

When you stop drinking, you have to get acceptance. That was something I wasn't able to apply in the business, but you really need it, a hundred percent. You have to accept the employees and who they are. You have to accept that even if you train your staff, they won't learn everything right away. Also, I had to accept that I couldn't do it alone.

I can't do it all. I can't be the dishwasher, the cook, the chef, the hostess, the waiter, the bartender. So, I accepted that other people could do it, probably not like I can do it, but they can do it well enough. Sometimes, you have to accept the unacceptable coming from the employees; they betray you, they steal, and you have to accept that. In business, I think it's important to know that you can be right, and you can have visions, but you've got to allow mistakes. If you make other people right, I think that's how you build a team. It's the employees that produce the food, and to produce the food, it's a team effort because you're manufacturing and retailing at the same time. So, the two teams, the team of manufacturing and team of retail, they've got to be in sync.

The other thing is, I couldn't have built this business without my family!

I couldn't because when I started, I was drinking. I had my brother and my brother-in-law with me, there was a lot of support, and they were my hands in a way. They were my hands and my legs because when I didn't get out of bed to open, they would do it. When I didn't do the preparation, they did it. When I was sleeping behind the counter, they kicked the door open. So, I know I could never have done it without them. They obviously knew the situations and as time went on, I stopped drinking.

I started clearing up my mind and I started to pay attention to what was out there and what was in the market and what people did. It was like an awakening. I started doing different things, and started focusing, promoting it in a way. I started the second restaurant. It became difficult to work with my family; I was moving too fast, and they were getting concerned, and because I was building the business in a different way than when I was drinking, they had questions, disagreements.

And so, I started opening the second restaurant with my two brothers. We opened the second restaurant with 33 percent each. And then we reopened the third in Vienna with a couple of employees we met as partners, but it didn't work, so we bought them out. And then my brother-in-law came from Italy, and he took 25 percent. I started realizing that it was harder for me to run my family than run my business. I could promote the business, but I couldn't promote my family with it, you know, changing prices, adding and removing stuff on the menu. I had a conflict; they didn't want to change things, they wanted to keep everything the same. That was a difficult time for me, and I started going on my own.

Over the years, I think it was important that my family, with my brothers and sister, we might disagree in business, we might disagree in a lot of things, to do or not do something, but we never disagreed on being a family. We were always a family.

Lillo was the one who actually backed me up more than my older brother, Vinny, and my brother-in-law, Fortunato. So again, we might have had some agreements and disagreements, some in partnership, not in partnership, close or open, but the family was always first.

My brother-in-law was a partner in the Vienna restaurant. We partnered in the real estate for the Vienna place, and we lease it to somebody else now. It's an English pub in the bottom floor and an office on the second floor.

I'm at peace with my brothers, my family. My brothers are my partners and I'm still in business with them, but in a way, I'm doing my own stuff. And I'm at peace with them because I did the best I could to run the business and maintain the family. I think they did the best they could.

Thirteen

You know, since I'm Sicilian, people always ask me about the Mafia. There has never been anybody that has come to me and asked for anything. I've never been approached. It's criminal.

In New York, in Chicago, these places, I understand the Portuguese, they control the concrete. But I think it's misunderstood. What it is, they have a great share of the market, and they get good prices. And I don't think people will go outside of that market. My thought, my understanding, in New York, is that the olive oil business and the trash collection business, whatever they started, they're working on it, and they didn't want the competition; they were scared of competition.

Now we have different kinds of problems than we had then. Now, I hear a company is too big and it can do what it wants. For me, that's Mafia too. A company like Twitter, Facebook, they shut people down. That's Mafia. If you want to talk about the Sicilian Mafia, this is the way they were too. It's illegal. I have my opinion, but I don't want to talk about it.

In the '70s, when somebody asked me, I would say I was Italian. Because if I were saying Sicilian, it's like a stigma. Me, I just want to make us better, but people will say, "This is the reason why they have what they have, because they're Mafia." Which is a way of saying, "Man, they can do it; but I can't do it." Which takes us to the essence of what I've been talking about. If you really want it, then you have to go for it. And you stay with it until you get it. But if you quit before you get it, that's like saying, "Well, they were lucky," or "It was easier before."

What I know is that I've been in business since 1978, and since 1978, my goal was always to do better. When I look at my business, I look at my competition, and I never get jealous. I was always like, why do they do better than me? Is it the location, the product? What is it?

So today, I'm working with my head down; I keep my side of the street clean; I still do what I had to do for years. Yes, I made mistakes, but I see today I'm getting all those rewards. For example, we have the Italy-America Chamber of Commerce. Two years ago, I got an award from them for being one of the best restaurants. But it's not because I'm doing anything different than I did before. I work. Today it's more outside the kitchen, and promoting, but it's still work!

Now, famous people make it to my restaurant. The stars, journalists, politicians, actors. Recently, we were named one of the best restaurants and pizzerias in Washington, D.C. We were one of the 70 best restaurants and pizzeria in the world. The week before we got *Travel & Leisure* magazine, and they said we were the best place to go in D.C. Sometimes I think, "Why didn't I get these awards before?" I was really dying for those things, 10, 20 years ago. I would see people getting them, and I was like, "How do you do it?"

I think it happens because I wouldn't quit; I show up and I'm here. Yesterday, I got really emotional; I was named one of the best restaurants in Washington D.C. by ESKCA.com, a top-rated restaurant website. My wife said, "You're not a quitter; you're strong, you just go!"

I'm 69 years old, and I started up a brand-new concept called 90 Second Pizza. Somebody said, "Oh, no, you're lucky. You got it because you started a long time ago." No, no. That's not true. What I'm doing is, I'm evaluating the good and the bad.

For example, when you sign a lease, you can give your life away if you make the wrong move. So, if I see a possibility, I go. I don't see a possibility, I won't go; I'll wait for the next one. And there's always a next one. There's an opportunity every day.

When I open a restaurant, I feel like it's going to be successful. I need to be in a place where people can park cars, walk; I need people living there, people shopping there, people working there. There is a community of people, and I want to reach them. And then, I need a good product.

Then, I design a look. For me, you don't want to look very expensive, you want to be comfortable, a warm place that's friendly. The design is just comfortable and not luxury. Everyday people can afford to come in.

Then there's the room itself. My idea, when I was setting up Joe's Place was, I designed a beautiful building to the best of my ability, using whatever money I could afford at the time to make it look inviting. There are a lot of regulations that limit you for signage, lighting, so you have to work with that. You've got to get permits, follow the local laws, a lot of that, and things slow you down.

And one thing that I did when I opened a new Joe's Place was I put up a big sign with a 50-foot crane, and the sign said, "Free Buffet, Free Pizza, and Pasta." And I had this big fork, it was like 10 feet tall, and some big, long tubes that waved in the air with blowers, so in the end it looked like spaghetti. And I would promote like this for two days, and I'd have a line around the building. Those days, I will serve maybe 500 to 1,000 people a day, and everybody gets to taste my product.

It's really free. The customers don't pay. Those two days, you get everything for free. You don't get a check. People come in;

the place will be full all day from 10 in the morning to 10 at night. If we get a line, we will put pizza in the buffet, salad, we'll keep everything. But for those two days, you don't get a check. You eat and go; I had that going. And I had more than 1,000 people tasting my food. I never calculated how much it costs. I got a recognition in the neighborhood; everybody was talking about it.

Sometimes, I will publicize in the newspaper, or I'll put an ad on the Internet, or I'll put a sign up on the building saying, "Great food, open today, free buffet." I will test all my equipment, I mean all the plumbing and the computers, to make sure everything works because my waiters, they will put out a check, but the check will come out zero. And it helps because inside, the drinks, preparation, the pizza guy, we're turning a switch so everybody will learn what to do. And you know what? If we make mistakes, it's for free; they'll forgive you.

And then, the third day, I will switch over, and I will start doing business. Other businesses, they just open the door, and it takes six months to a year to get to where we are already!

A lot of people, for lunch, they wanted to be served fast, and they ordered different things. One wants pasta, one wants lasagna, one wants a sandwich. You need a lot of manpower to do all that. So, after about six months, a friend of mine suggested that we do a buffet. And how did we promote the buffet? We made a sign that took one side of the building. From the end of the building to the front of the building, and when people were going to work in Arlington, they saw our sign: Lunch $3.99! And we had a couple of specials, too, if you don't want the buffet. So, then we started the buffet, which was a tremendous success!

When you open a business, you've got to go as big as you can, make as much noise as you can, not just talk loud in silent places. People within a couple of miles away, they have to hear you, and they've got to see you. They're going to notice you; that's how you're going to sell. Because if nobody knows you, you can have the best product in the world, it won't sell, and it will spoil. You need people to know about it. What do you have to do? Advertisement is expensive. Those days, we had the coupon books. Buy one, get one free. I mean, that was also a way to bring people in and taste the product. What I think is, with promotion like that, my business will grow, and people will come back.

And one thing, the bathroom is essential; the bathroom should be sparkling. It should be cleaned not daily, but hourly. Windows should be without fingerprints.

The waiters should be pleasant and should be in nice, clean uniforms. If they don't come to work with clean uniforms, you send them home to get cleaned up and come back. And you don't sit down with the customers to take an order. Never turn your back to the customer; you turn your back to the kitchen. Pay attention to the people. Don't make the customer invisible. The customers, when they turn around, they should get the waiter's attention.

A lot of times when you go to a restaurant, nobody knows you, it's like you're invisible. Make them visible, that's why we are here, to serve the customer. He comes, he wants to sit down within a reasonable time, he wants you to take his order, he wants a clean place. He wants to order, he wants to get what he ordered, and after he finishes, he wants to get his bill, and he wants to pay. That's what is expected. When you come in, welcome; when you leave, thank you.

Make your customer feel like you appreciate him, and they will appreciate you. You do that by providing a clean place, good service, good product, and value for the money. That's what I think and I'm an expert, a person that knows the restaurant business.

I am not an artist in cooking; I'm a trained pizza man. From when I was 17 until about 40, I made pizza every day. I was pretty much the heart of the product of Joe's Place. I worked seven years for others before I started my own business. But I am not a great chef. I like food, I like to eat, I like all kinds of food. I don't care about more expenses, and I don't really go for that.

Some people, they could have money to do a restaurant, because they like to cook. They might be doctors, lawyers, construction guys, professionals. And they get into this fantasy that because they know how to cook, they can have their own restaurant. They get the second trust, and they put a restaurant together. It looks good, and they spend a lot of money. And when they open it and cook a good meal, nobody comes in. Why? Because nobody knows.

So, in all my years' experience, I learned you've got to make some noise here. Before opening, after opening, now today because I'm more known, and the media are watching me. Every time I make a move, or open a restaurant, or someone well-known comes to il Canale, the media is there. I think that's dangerous; they can do bad things and good things, you know? If you make a stupid move, they can hurt you, too. So, it's funny. Before, when I needed media attention, I never got it; now, I got it, and I don't even need it. Media is always good, that's what they say.

I think you can build a nice, good location; you can build and make it a destination. If you have good service and good food... I've come to believe that service is more important than food, and location is more important than food and service. So, all those three things, I think, location, quality, and service. You need more advertising if you have a bad location. In the market, an average chain, a big international chain, it spends millions and millions on advertising. I never spent that. Me, now, I don't spend a penny on advertising. I pay a PR firm, virtual digital guy, $400 a month to operate my website. When we get emails or comments, we have people look at it. I paid a lot more advertising when I was running Joe's Place. There was a period of time that I was on cable TV, and did coupons, and had ads in the *Washington Post*. I was spending a lot on advertising. But of course, at that time, we were doing good sales at Joe's Place. Now we spend a lot less than two, three percent. A national company, it bombards you, they do a million-dollar promotion like it's nothing.

When I had five Joe's Place, we were grossing about six, seven million in all the locations, and had about 150 people working. So, that was costing probably $100,000 a year in advertising out of six million, but the advertising that I did, I always made sure it was effective. I see a lot of people advertising ten or twenty percent off the cost of a meal. And that brings in maybe three people. If you put an ad in the paper, it'll cost you $1,000, and you might get five new customers. But if you spend $1,000 and you do a *buy one, get one free* campaign, you might get 100 people. That 100 people, they're going to bring you more than $1,000.

Advertising, sometimes it's not effective. It's like you're trying to trick the customers.

The advertising needs to be effective the way you want it to be. Like, I don't want to do tricks when I do an ad. I think I'm an honest person. If you are trying to sell me something, and you're tricking me, I'll hate you; I won't come back. I scratch you off the list, because tricking me, it means you think I'm stupid. So, I think in advertising, if you do it, it needs to be honest. I'll give the customer a deal, for real; you give them a discount that time and not forever. I mean, yeah, I want you to try my food, and I'll give it to you for 50 percent off, or buy two; you and your friend come, one pays, and one is free. So you try it and now two people are trying my product. I trust my product, and you're trusting my product; I trust in my cleanliness; I trust my location; I trust in the place and the service that I'm going to give you. Those three things are going to make it desirable for you to come back. You have to give the customer something real.

People are not stupid. They've been tricked too many times. Some major chains do that; you know what I mean? "Oh, $10 off, $3 off. get the third one free…" I can't figure it out.

The game is not that we take the customers' money, but that they want to come back. It's got to be the customer because he's going to analyze things. He's going to think, "If I go there, I'm going to get a nice meal, it's going to be fair, I'm going to be served well by a nice person. Why would I want to go to another place where nobody knows me, the bathrooms are dirty, I have to wait to get seated."

My thing is, I want to make it easy, as easy as I can from my 50 years' experience. What I see when I go to a restaurant, I see what I *don't* want to do; all the stuff that inconveniences me.

It's not enough that you want to open a place because you're a good cook. If you're a lawyer, if you're an investor, how do you know all these things I've been talking about? You don't, and that's why the chance of failure is really high. Because it's not like you want to sell bicycles, so you open a bicycle store, and you sell them for cheap, and you get more customers, and you buy and sell. Same thing for concrete, or tiles, gold; that stuff doesn't go out of style, and it doesn't spoil.

If you sell gold, it actually increases in price. In the restaurant, it's not the same. Product spoils if you're not prepared. Also, buying the product is important. When you buy, you think you're buying from a company that's good and a month later, you see a product is five or ten percent more expensive. What do you do? You have two or three companies and you're buying and trying to compare prices of the same product, exactly the same product.

If you're lazy and you don't know, you buy everything from one company. Your food costs two, three percent more, and that costs you your profit.

Fourteen

I designed my logos with the help of graphic designers. The last two logos for the most recent restaurants were designed by my son, Roberto, who graduated from Pratt School of Design in New York.

Then, what's important is that the name says something about what you are going to sell and who you are. Some restaurants can have the first or last names of people. It's good when you're known. You know, the thing about Italian, any name looks good and sounds good if it finishes with O, with E, or with A. The name is very, very important.

My first place, I was working in a restaurant that was named Guy's Place, so, I named my restaurant Joe's Place. I think, if it worked for him, it'd work for me. And then, I put Joe's Place Pizza and Subs.

I didn't want to do my Italian name, Giuseppe. Giuseppe is more restaurant than pizza place. It's more silverware, more china, more wine. My beginning, I was pizza and subs, and it worked really well. I was giving quality, but I didn't want to sound expensive. So, the name sometimes, tells the message; tells us who you want to be.

We are coming out of a pandemic, and I think 30 percent of the restaurants, they're not going to survive this. And Joe's, was one of them. We wouldn't survive because, mostly, we had the lunch buffet where you can come in and eat. We were doing fine; it was profitable; we made a good living. And if it wasn't for the pandemic, we'd still be Joe's, we wouldn't have changed to A Modo Mio. So, I wanted to make that clear, and now we're in the position to get back in the market.

Now it's hard to find employees. The government kept it at 50 percent capacity for a while, so people did not go out. But I think, soon we're going to have more people in here; people are going to feel more relaxed about going out to eat. It's all mental if you're vaccinated.

I think we're going to be fine. It's been good to get help from the government; the Payroll Protection Plan (PPP), helped us a lot. Without that, we would have been in survival mode, maybe not making it. But this way, we were going to be covered until July 2021 with PPP money, and that's a spectacular thing. It covered the payroll; it covered the rent and the utility for 25 weeks. Within 25 weeks, we were out of this, and business was okay. We're working one customer at a time, thinking about making one customer happy; the customers will multiply eventually. Just give them a nice clean place and really good service.

In this area, the average family income is pretty high, I think, so we're in the right place. People living here, they want this. It's a necessity for them. There's a lot of places, Domino's, Papa John's, they're making pizza using the frozen dough, canned tomato that are already seasoned, processed cheese. We don't do this. For A Modo Mio, we buy quality flour. Our flours are organic, Italian wheat. It's not genetically altered; it has no chemicals at all.

In other restaurants, maybe all those Italian pastas, they're coming from Italy, but the wheat to make them, it comes from America or Canada and is shipped over there, and it gets grinded. They make pizza flour and they call it Italian flour, which it's not.

They can still say it comes from Italy because I think they use a percentage to mix it, not a big percentage, but a tiny one that they manufacture, and they call it imported from Italy.

The food we make is authentic Italian. We make pizza the way pizza was originally made, the old way in Napoli. We use Italian flour. The tomatoes were grown in the area where pizza was invented, and the *bufala* mozzarella is not regular cow milk; it's *buffalo*. They're not originally Italian, they were brought over from America a long time ago. And then there's the weather, and what they're eating. They produce a special kind of milk.

So, we are a Mediterranean restaurant, but basically, pizza is our flag, and it is Neapolitan pizza. It was made for Queen Margarita. They made a pizza with white and red and green. Red tomato, white mozzarella, the green was the basil. It represented the Italian flag. So, from then, pizza stayed in Italy, in Naples for about 100 years. With the TV, with radios, pizza started travelling outside the city, and it traveled all over Italy. But every place it traveled to, they changed it; they made it fit the flour, they made it fit their tomato, they made it fit the olive oil, they made it fit whatever ingredients they had.

In the mid 1900s, after World War II, it left Italy and it came to America. The American soldiers, when they came back home, they'd go to the Italian restaurant and ask, "You're making a pizza?" The Italian people, though, they lived in America, and they didn't even know what pizza was. The soldiers, they explained it to them. "Oh, it's like bread, with sauce on top." And the Italian-Americans were trying to make it, basically how the American soldier told them to.

That's why there are so many kinds of pizza in America: Chicago, New York, California, whatever.

But here, we are back to basics. It's fresh, but it's the old way. By using an oven that goes to about 900 degrees, we cook a pizza in 60 to 90 seconds, and the pizza will never be crispy; it will be juicy and tender. We recommend you use a fork and knife, or you can fold it, like Neapolitans do. I've been doing Neapolitan pizza now for about 10 years, 11 years. I've done New York style for 40 years, and I have to retrain my customers. So, I told my waiters and the cashiers, before they take an order for pizza, I say, "Please ask the clients if they've ever had a Neapolitan pizza before." Because if they haven't, they'll be surprised; it's completely different. And so, we've been educating our customers. But our customers multiply, you know, they're growing, and that means we keep making more and more pizza, and it requires very skilled people to make them. So, it's really a lot of training to teach a pizza man to work with this oven. It takes six months to a year to make him skilled. And you pay them more because they are skilled artisans.

I'm a little bit of a fanatic because I like to do it. For me, food is food, even if it's cheap food, you do the best you can. I like to have my human experience in it and use a really original product.

I want to note a few things that changed my life. One is, when I decided that I want to be in the pizza business, how that came about. The other one, was when I decided to stop drinking. A third one was when I realized I was doing this business already; I was in business for maybe three, four, or five years, but I was making pizza for about 12 years when I opened a restaurant in Bailey's Crossroad.

A couple of blocks down the road, there was another pizzeria owned by a Greek. I had a customer come in to eat at my place every day, and we become friends. He said, "You know, Joe, that other pizzeria, they used to make a good pizza. But in the last couple of years, they don't make a good pizza anymore."

I said to him, "No, they made the same pizza two years ago. Now you tried a better product, you went back and tasted their pizza, and you thought, 'They changed the recipe!' But no, they didn't change their recipe; you changed your palate—because you improved your palate and then came back to the pizza you're used to." It's just like driving your Chevrolet, then you go drive a Mercedes. It doesn't mean the Chevrolet isn't good anymore; no, the car is still good. You've changed."

That was one thing the customers told me: That I was a little bit above the normal way of doing things, because my goal is to make the best pizza in the world. And that's been very costly, with a lot of stress because I want to go all the way; I always want to improve. If you talk to my pizza guys, you talk to my manager, my slogan is, "We are good, but we can always do better."

You know, at the start, I only knew how to make pizza; I didn't have any idea how everything was going to come out. So, I figured I'd just go cheap, good, simple, clear; everything is to be as normal as possible. I didn't make a statement. For me, it was just the name; I didn't think the logo was important. But over the years, I realized the name Joe's, it's all over the place and that's when I realized that the name was important.

The reason I picked the name il Canale for the restaurant in Georgetown was because, yes, it's right near the C & O Canal, but also because there was no restaurant named that. I put the blue line under the logo: *il Canale <u>Georgetown</u>*.

And then, I opened 90 Second Pizza. Why did I name it 90 Second? Because the pizza is fast. People ask me, "So, you make pizza in 90 seconds?" I say, "Yes." So, speed, and I'm selling quality and innovation and tradition. So, the name fits with the speed, the speed fits with the price, you have a winning combination.

Why did I call the new restaurant A Modo Mio? It means, "my way" in Italian. A Modo Mio, it's me; my way, my way to run the business. If you want to do it my way, we do it. I would have called it Bella Vita, but that was a more generic name with a lot of places called Bella Vita.

A Modo Mio, it's where the Joe's Place Pizza and Pasta used to be. The locals are probably learning about it; not everybody, but a lot of people, they come here, and they look disoriented when they walk in, and they're like, "Where is the buffet?" And when they don't see the buffet, they walk right out, because they have something in their mind that they expected.

So you turn the page, and you're going to be A Modo Mio now, you can't be Joe's. People come because they trust Joe, and now they trust A Modo Mio.

Joe's Place died. Really, that's the best way to explain it. The COVID killed the restaurant. Joe's was an old concept, from the '70s and I got 40 years out of it. After the divorce, I started closing all the Joe's Place, and the last one was finished off by COVID.

So I've been doing the new concept with il Canale in Georgetown for 11 years. When I came from Italy and started working with pizza shops, I was the dishwasher and the cleaning boy, and I already had the desire to succeed, wanting to do something. I talked about the time when the pizza man I was working with, he went to the bathroom and an order came in, and I did it myself. That was probably a very special moment for my career.

I could've said, "I don't care, let me wait for him to come out of the bathroom," but I wanted to learn. I saw that there was a place for me to improve, and I could earn more money. And then, from there, because I had the desire to do better, that was something very critical. It couldn't have happened when I went to drive a taxi, or when I was painting, when I was working in a body shop. Pizza did it. I took pizza that was already there, and I brought it here.

One of the joys was learning the pizza thing, the other, was the choice to say no to my whole drinking life, and to say yes to a 12-step meeting. And then, another thing is that I don't take no for an answer.

When I was going to open the third Joe's in Arlington, I knew the place was available, and I called the company. I made them an offer because the rent was low; I was excited. And then, I asked a friend of mine who has a restaurant, "What do you think about this place?" He says, "The former restaurant there didn't make it; it's a bad location. Because if they failed, you're going to fail, too."

I get that all the time in business, that people say you can't do this or that. All my restaurants that I opened; they all were where other people failed. I made them successful.

For me, it's not the location that fails, it's the management, it's the leadership that fails. If the leader did not have a vision, and didn't have a product, didn't have a location, didn't have a logo, didn't have a menu, didn't have all those things, you have nothing. I believe that.

Not every location is good for everything. There are locations you can sell cars, jewelry, hardware, food, or bicycles.

A restaurant needs to have the best scenario; you want to have parking, visibility, people can walk to it, they can ride to it. Lots of people living nearby, or near a college. That will be the best location. To have all that, you have to pay a premium per square foot. There are a lot of locations like this in the city, where you have people right there, so that's why you pay a lot of money in rent. But if you don't want to pay a premium, then you've got to be smart.

I usually think if those chains like McDonald's or Burger King, Pizza Hut, Red Lobster, whatever, if they're making it, if you're within a block or two of them, you can make it, too. There's no bad location if you're a block away from McDonald's. But bad location for me, they don't exist. It's the ideas, the leader, the management, the food, that make it work.

I had to learn that talking to negative people, it gives you fear because they give you their negativity, and I had to stay with my own belief that I am one of the best pizza makers in the world.

I know how to make a good product; I'm really educated in what I do. I know how to sell it myself: I know I've done it many times, and I pick good locations. A lot of times, you get up in the morning, you talk to somebody, you try to do something, and they say, "Oh no, everyone else is failing there." I have to say, "Yeah, they failed, but there's got to be a reason." A lot of restaurants, they're going to be failing because they were sick already. Just like COVID hit people that already have multiple health problems. Restaurants like that, they were barely breaking even, or they already were losing money.

Me, I bet it all because I know I'll do better, and I believe that I can do it, and I make the bet. It's not like betting on the stock market or playing cards. I'm betting on me, my capacity. I've proved that I could make a good product; my customers, they loved it, and they love the place where I work, so it turned out to be a big deal.

My bosses in the early days, some of them were workaholics; some of them stupid; some of them had no manners; they were like, dirty. Some of them, they didn't know what we were doing, and some of them survived anyway, they were successful somehow, as successful as they wanted to be. But I wanted to be more successful. I wanted the American dream, I want it, I want it. I saw that it's possible here in America to do what you want, America will push you in the right place, will size you. The demand will size you, will accept you or not accept you. And that's what I've been learning more about: that the time when I got started, my desire, my vision, my dream, I dreamed so much about what I wanted to do for myself. I was going into the unknown initially. I knew what I was going to do; I was going to make a pizza, the very best pizza, and people were going to love it.

And why not? Why are they not going to like mine? And then, when they started coming in, I started getting more encouraged, I started to get more creative, doing more things, and people liked that, too. In this business, what I will teach is this: If you do right, if you believe in it, and you're paying employees right; when you treat your employees right, when you treat your customers right, when you make the best product you can, you keep the place as clean as you can, and you price it the best you can, and as an old friend used to say, you deliver the goods, you'll get a reward. I've been doing more of that. As I'm getting more mature, growing older, I do more of the right things.

Fifteen

The story of my marriage to Teresa, it's beautiful. It took about three years to finally meet her and to be alone for dinner—but not for anything else.

I would go to Italy every summer, July and August. I was divorced already for about 15 years, and I noticed this beautiful woman, who had become a widow. She was really attractive. I knew her, I knew her husband, but we were not friends. It's a small village where I come from, Castrofillipo, and we all know each other.

And so, I told my cousin, I said, "Caterina, do you know if Teresa's seeing anybody? I know she lost her husband." And my cousin says, "No, she doesn't see anybody." So, I asked my cousin to get us together, and we went to the beach.

So me, her, my cousin, her cousin, we were like, five. Her kids came too, so we weren't alone. And I was trying to get her attention, but she didn't even notice me.

A year passed, I was there in the summer again, we went to the beach again. Same thing: no interest, no noticing me. It was just like, people you know, friends. My cousin, her best friend. Me, I'm American, let's go to the beach.

In year number three, I called her, and I asked, "Can we have coffee together?" And she says, "No, no way." But by now, I really was interested in her; I really liked her.

So, I did not take no for an answer. I went back to my cousin again and said, "Let's all go for dinner!" And my cousin, she asked Teresa, and she said no. Her reason was that she was a widow, and she did not want anything to do with another man. She became a widow when she was about 46. She had two girls; the youngest was a student at the university in Bologna, and the oldest worked. So, Teresa was being the mother and father. She didn't put her head up; she just put her head down and did what she had to do. During this time, I would call her more often, but she really expressed that she was not interested, she said she really didn't have another life in her plans. She's just going to support her kids, and just stay in town and not marry.

But I persuaded her. I said, "You're young, gorgeous, you have a life to live, I mean, you're going to experience a lot of things."

Anytime I called her, she was really nervous. Even though she answered the phone, she wasn't giving me much attention. But then, one day she told me that every time I called her, she was terrified because she didn't want to change; she wanted to stay the same, and I was sort of a threat, trying to make a change in her life.

About this time, year number three, after we get a little more acquainted by phone, I started sending flowers once a week, and she started panicking and then, I think I sent her a song, an Italian song, *Io Ci Saro,* and she told me every time she listened to that song, she became a little more open to me.

One time, in the spring, me, my cousin, and her, we went for lunch. And I said, "I really want to get something started with you. I'm not trying to play; I'm serious".

After we finished lunch, she tells me—and that was something that kept me up—she says, "Having lunch with you today, it was like cheating on my husband." By this time, her husband has been gone five, six years. And she said, "Well, if you want to be friends, we can stay friends, you can call me for Christmas."

In my mind, I'm like, "Yeah, sure." I need another girlfriend that I could call for Christmas. But I said, "Yes, fine. Okay, understood." I thought she wasn't ready. I thought, "You know what? Forget it. I'm not going to lose any more time and effort here." My feelings were hurt, and there was nothing happening, and I understood that I had to move on or lose more. So, I left it there at lunch. You know, I accepted it, and I'm thinking, "You know what? Forget it. If she thinks that way, I don't want to keep going."

I went to Italy again in the summertime. I went to my cousin's. I'm very close with my cousin. My mom lived at my cousin's house for about 12 years when she moved back to Italy. They pretty much adopted her, and usually when I go to Italy, the first thing I do, I go see my cousin.

I went there and I wasn't thinking about Teresa because I thought it was over. I didn't want to impose, I wanted to be respectable, I didn't want to be overreaching and I said so. Then as I was leaving, my cousin Caterina says, "Do you know that Teresa is upset? She's mad at you."

I'm surprised, "Why?"

My cousin says, "You never call her anymore."

"I thought she was not done with her grief, so, I stayed away!"

"Well," my cousin says, "she thought you were going to call her. When you didn't call over the holidays, it proved to her you were not very serious."

I had thought it was over already, I mean, there was nothing there but whatever was my part. And right there, now I'm thinking, "Wow! Maybe she is interested after all!"

So, I called her, and said, "Hi, I'm here." And that summer we spent more time together, but never alone, always with my cousin. She doesn't want to be seen with anybody. Especially, with me because I live in America. She was not sure yet; she wanted to get to know me first before she would make a commitment.

I didn't have any issues; she had issues. She didn't want to be seen. I was ready to meet a woman, but she was very conservative, and she didn't want people to talk about her, because people talk about things in Sicily, in my town, when they see something different.

We were going different places for dinner, always with my cousin, and when we got out of town, Teresa would come and sit in the front seat, and when we returned to town, she changed seats with my cousin. It was funny. We were like kids. That summer went well; we got to spend more time together and got to know each other in a friendly way, and nobody knew. I don't think she even told her mom then; she told her mom later.

I said to her, "Please, before you commit, come to America, stay in my house, I have an extra room."

But I told her that I was very serious in the relationship; I wasn't playing. I really liked her, and I wanted her to get to know me more, get to know my life, and what I do. Get to know my family, my friends.

She already knew my kids. My kids grew up next door to where she lived, her sister lives there. The families live next to each other, and they had boys. So my kids, every summer they came, they were good friends. They knew Teresa's daughters, they know the cousins. I mean, they hang around, especially Roberto; he would stay over with friends and spend time there.

So Teresa accepted my offer to come and visit me in America. I said, "I'll send you a ticket," which was the wrong thing to say. She felt insulted; "You're not going to pay for my ticket. I can afford to buy my ticket!"

I said, "Fine. As long as you come here, so you get to know if you'll like what I'm doing. If you don't like it, maybe it'll help you to make a decision."

So finally, I convinced her to come. She came in June, a week before my birthday. I showed her the Italian church where we went to mass on Sunday, and then we went to il Canale. I invited my family to meet her, and a couple of my friends. On my birthday, I thought about giving her a present; I got a ring, just a little ring, and I said, "I just wanted to give you a present, so that you don't forget about me." I gave her the ring, but she didn't want to accept it. She says, "I'm not ready to make a decision. I'm not ready to decide if I want to change my life, if I want to be here." I tell her, "It's for friendship."

She went back to Sicily, and I persuaded her to visit me in September for a month with her two daughters. She didn't tell anybody, not even her mom, and I don't know if she told her sister,

I'm sure if Teresa tells the story, it will be different for her.

Eventually she told her mom, "Hey mom, I met somebody!" And the mom says, "Oh, my beautiful daughter, I am so happy, I've been praying for you that you'll meet somebody, and you'll be happier, so you don't have to be alone."

And then Teresa says, "Yes, mom, but he lives in America." And the mom's face changed, and she didn't talk about it for about two months. So, Teresa had to work with that, and then, she talked to the sisters and the brothers-in-law. And pretty much, she came to the decision that she was interested, she wanted to continue the relationship.

She had met my friend, Melo Cicala, that week in 2015 when she came here, and Melo said that I recently had built a brand-new kitchen, a brand-new bathroom and everything in my house in McLean. But it turns out Teresa tells Melo she would like to live in Georgetown!

I say, she never told me that. She didn't say that she didn't like McLean, but she doesn't speak English, she doesn't drive, and everything in Georgetown is close by, which will be better. He says, "There's a house in my block for sale!" So, I went to look at it, but I didn't like it. Then I started looking and found my house, where we live now.

I saw the house was for sale, it has a view of the Potomac River, and I called the real estate agent right away. I said, "Please, you're going to help me to get this house because I love it; I want a house with a view."

It wasn't easy, but we made the deal, and I got the house. There was some financial stress, but everything worked out. In October 2015, I called Teresa in Sicily and I said, "Hey, I bought a house in Georgetown, and I'll send you some pictures. You never told me that you wanted to live in the city, but Melo told me!"

She tells me. "I didn't want you to buy a house!"

I said, "Well yeah, I would like you to live in the city…"

In November, I moved from McLean to Georgetown. She came again around Christmas time with her kids. One girl went back, and the other girl stayed longer because she had already finished school and graduated. Teresa and Dalila started going to school together to learn English.

On February second, 2016, we got married in City Hall in D.C. because I wanted to get the documents for the immigration started.

That was another thing. I thought it was like, we go there, we fill out a license and we get married. Luckily, I took Melo and Dalila, and they were our witnesses. I wasn't even dressed up. I picked Teresa up from school, she changed, and at that time, I thought, "This is very, very serious stuff! We just got married, and we should throw a party!" So, we threw a party for about 100 people. We put the party together in three days and it was spectacular. My kids were there. Dalila was here; the other girl, Manuela, she was in Italy. One of the guests was Joe Coleman, the singer from The Platters, who sang *Only You* to Teresa and me.

Earlier in 2015, while Teresa was in Italy, I went to North Carolina. A friend of mine is a pilot, and we leased a plane. I went to see a business opportunity. I phoned Teresa and told her, "When I come back to Italy, I want us to get a plane and pilot and take us on a flight over Sicily. Will you like that?" She told me she would.

This was how I was going to propose to her. I would propose on the plane; I'd ask her, "*Teresa, mi vuoi sposare?*" Which is "Would you marry me?" in Italian. We would fly over my village, at 200 meters. I had that all planned.

I went to Italy in May 2015, and I organized the pilot and an enormous sign with 15-foot letters saying, *Teresa, mi vuoi sposare?* She didn't know anything about it. I said, "You remember when I told you I was going to take you in a plane and take a ride around Sicily?"

She really didn't want to; she was a little scared and nervous getting on a small plane. Once again, she didn't tell anybody that I was taking her up in a plane, except for her daughters, and that was in case the plane crashed.

We went up in the air from Catania. It turns out that day, there was a military exercise somewhere nearby and we were told we could not go through; we cannot go there.

I said, "No, we've got to go there!" Teresa was saying, "It's okay, we don't have to. We'll go somewhere else!"

I said, "No, I want to go to Castrofilippo, that's where I want to go!" But the pilot already knew why I wanted to go there. I had the huge sign in a field, on my brother-in-law's land, with the 15-foot letters.

Teresa's niece, she's an architect, had designed the layout. And my friend, Angelo, he was the one that installed the sign with his son while I was driving to the airport. All this stuff was coming together at this point. And I forgot my passport! Good thing the pilot was an instructor, so he got us in like we were students.

So, we get in the plane, and the tower said, "You have to delay because of this military exercise." Twenty minutes later, they say we can go, and we get near my town. By the way, I had already bought a diamond ring that I was going to give to her.

There's a lake we flew over. And I see the sign and say, "Teresa, look down there!"

She saw the sign and she started screaming! And then, at the same time, I get the ring and I say, "Teresa, will you marry me?"

She kept screaming, she was so excited. I said, "You don't like the ring?"

She says, "Yes, yes, I will marry you!".

After that, we flew at 200 meters over the Agrigento Greek temples with the plane almost skimming the top, which was illegal. I wanted to fly above my village, but I was so excited I forget to tell the pilot.

We get back to Catania airport and I had secretly organized catering with my friends and family. We have about 50 people. We had catering at Giovanna's, Teresa's sister. We organized the catering, and I had ordered 100 roses with the message, *Per Sempre,* Forever, in Italian.

That day, there was also my son, Alessandro, who was in Italy on vacation, and Teresa's daughters, Dalila and Manuela. There was a lot of family there with flags. I had told Teresa, "I don't want to go home, let's go to Giovanna's and spend time with our family. They must be excited for us, because they know that I was going to propose to you."

So, when we went back, all my guests, all my family and Teresa's family, everybody, was already there. The flowers were there. Teresa, she was blown away. That moment, my mother-in-law, she was very happy too. She started grabbing me, kissing me, hugging me; she fell in love with me. It was like, Teresa's whole family embraced me.

I didn't stay in Sicily long; I was there for one week. I just went there to propose because she already had met my family.

In August 2016, we went back, and we got married in Taormina, because I had my kids and my brother Vinny, his wife Rosa, and friends from America who came to the wedding, as well as friends that came from all over Italy. I wanted to get married somewhere where they could come for the weekend, they would get entertained.

We had a bus from the village to Taormina for people that couldn't drive. The rest came with their cars, plus the guests that were staying there.

This waiter, he worked in il Canale in D.C., as well as in Taormina. So, he knew the hotel, he knew the manager, and Teresa, she organized the wedding on the phone with this lady manager. So, we got our flowers and the photographer, and we did the wedding with about 130 people. I think it was the most beautiful wedding I have ever been to.

A year before, in 2015, I had met Tom Sinatra at il Canale. He is a famous guitarist from Sicily. Because we were from the same city, we connected. So, after lunch I said, "I'll take you to the airport!" On the way, my friend, Melo, said, "Do you know how Joe proposed to his future wife, Teresa?"

Melo started telling the story to Sinatra, who says, "I'm going to be in your wedding. I'm going to play guitar for you!"

He says, "I think I read about your proposal to your fiancée in the newspaper." There had been a write-up about it, a story about this not-so-young Italian living in America, who had come back to marry a local woman.

Some other papers must have picked it up because he knew. He said, "Yeah, I heard about that." And he promised me that he was going to play at the wedding.

On August 3, 2016, the night before the wedding, he called me. I said, "What's up with you? I never heard from you."

He says, "I really want to surprise you, but I need to know a little more in detail. Where is the wedding?" I was happy that he was going to be there because Tom is really one of the best guitarists in the world.

Finally, the wedding starts. Tom is also a pianist; he's a real musician; he sings, plays violin, guitar, and piano.

Teresa and I go to the hotel Capotaormina a day before with her girls. Two of my sons came, too. We went to church, and the church's air conditioning is broken; it's 95 degrees in there, and the air condition doesn't turn on until half the mass is over. We got a violinist to play and then, Tom comes in and gets on the piano, and it was beautiful.

After that, we go to the restaurant. The day before, I'd gone and talked to the hotel band and said, "Tomorrow I'm going to get married. I hope you guys are good because I want to enjoy myself. I have a special guest coming, Tom Sinatra!"

It turns out they know Tom! The bandleader tells me, "Me and Tom, we've done a lot of shows together!"

I said, "Don't tell anybody, I will announce it myself." So the guys got together, and with Tom they started jamming at the hotel. It was great music! We were dancing; it was hot and humid, a bunch of hotel guests joined us. This hotel is 200 to 300 feet above the water, and you can see the Mediterranean. I don't want to exaggerate, but it felt like being in Hollywood, like we were stars in the movies.

We didn't make a video of my wedding, but I have a lot of videos from friends.

Anyway, around 11 o'clock, I had organized fireworks to go off over the water. The hotel manager stops the music and announces, "We want everybody to go on the balcony." The fireworks set off. At the end, the shape of a heart lights up in the water. It lasted 20 minutes, and then everybody went back to dancing. We had the cake right near the pool…

After it all, I couldn't carry my wife into a room, I didn't want to hurt myself. I was 63 and that's how I got married.

We've been going back to Italy every year, except for last year because of COVID. For our first anniversary, we went there, and we were at the beach. It's a stone beach, you need shoes to walk. We got some sun, and there were two couples next to us.

I asked, "How long have you guys been here?"

They said, "We come every year. By the way, last year, we were here at the same time, and there was this spectacular wedding and fireworks."

It was our wedding. It's my story and I'm sticking to it!

Sixteen

I'm planning to open a 90 Second Pizza in Chinatown soon. We've signed a lease. We started the design and construction. That restaurant might take about eight months to open.

I negotiated with the owner of that property in Chinatown. It's on Seventh Street across from the Convention Center. Chinatown is disappearing, in a way. It's become a tourist place. There are very few Chinese restaurants left, and everybody's selling. The Chinese are selling to outside companies.

So, I was negotiating for a property, and we got to the place where I thought we agreed, and then there was something I didn't understand when we talked about triple net that was included in the price. Triple net means tax, insurance, and rent. Net, net, net. And that means all is included in the negotiated price. I said, "Now what?"

The difference was between $13,900 to $16,500 in monthly rent, or about $30,000 a year. That was the gap, and I said, "You know what? If you give it to me, I'll take it. If you're not going to give it to me for my price, I'm not going to take it."

They answered, "I don't think so."

I said, "Let's meet in the middle," and they accepted. That's a negotiation skill.

I have a real estate broker for commercial properties. I talk to him, and he helps with mediating with landlords. He gets paid by the landlord, which is how it is normally done in commercial real estate. If I don't get the property, he's not making anything in the deal; he's got to make both of us happy. He'll have to close the deal to get his commission.

There's too much demand for that property. Everybody wants to be there. Next to me, I have a local hamburger store, a Chipotle and then a Chick-fil-A; all the big boys…

It is one of the best locations in the city, with tourists, offices, the Convention Center, residential, everything's there. We're shooting to do double the sales that I do in Georgetown.

I have employees to help me develop the 90 Second Pizza idea. I have Antonio, a new Neapolitan pizza guy. He's going to be working for a regular salary, and he's going to be in the profit-sharing. I promised him I'm going to give him a percentage of the profit of the store.

He's going to be a pizza maker, and he's also got to train the future pizza man, then he's going to get himself a couple of assistants.

My son, Alessandro, is going to pay the rent, the payroll, the licensing.

I'm going to do it a different way. Antonio is quality control for the whole 90 Second concept. If I want to make an adjustment, I'll tell him a little more salt, a little more pepper. So, yeah, I am still involved. Like right now, this morning, I went to il Canale because the pizza oven there is leaking too much heat.

So, I had a metal guy come in this morning at 6:30 and put in insulation. I need a new bathroom in 90 Second, so I got another guy to do that.

Let's say maybe there's something wrong with the management, then I step into that area to find a solution. I trust my cook, I trust my pizza man, they have their soldiers in the right place. And then I check the product, the touch of tomato, of cheese, of flour. Yeah, the flour: I went to Italy and to the mill where they grind it. And I touched it when it came out of the machine; I smelled it, and it smelled wonderful, which is what I am looking for.

I'm an entrepreneurial pizza maker. I don't have the experience to do fine dining.

At il Canale, there was this friend of mine, I'd met him here at Joe's a couple of years before, and il Canale happened. So, this friend, he was living with a roommate from college, and I liked the way we connected. I had a nice house in McLean. I said to him, "You know what? I have an extra room. If you want it, you can stay in my house for maybe a week, a month, or whatever."

We had a lot of fun when he lived there. He was a guy's guy, you know what I mean? We had barbecue parties at the house. I mean, really fun. But then, it was too much, so he left, but we were still friends when he left the house.

A few years later, he said, "Hey, Joe, let's do the pizza in Neapolitan style." I didn't want any partners; I didn't want to do anything. Then he said, "There's this group, they have a bunch of pizzerias in Naples, and they have one in Miami; you should look into it because they're willing to partner with us."

I went to the place in Naples, checked it out, met the partners, they looked like nice people. We ended up forming a corporation that still exists to this day. We were supposed to be five partners, each of us was going to put $100,000, and we were going to open this franchise here in D.C.

But I asked my broker, "Do you have any locations?"

He says, "I have a place in Georgetown; we'll look at it."

The location used to be a Mexican restaurant, so my broker

negotiated a good deal to buy it. The other partners were looking for another location, but I didn't really like it, so I picked Georgetown for the franchise to move in there.

So, we're supposed to put $100,000 each; I put my $100,000, one of the partners puts $80,000. His good friend, who's supposed to put the deal together, he says he's selling his house, so after he sells it, he will be able to put in his percentage. And the other two partners, they say, "Well, we're going to be paying for the furniture, the pizza oven, and also, we're going to pay for the construction."

So, I worked out a deal with them. I was a silent partner. So, we used some of my money for the deposit to buy the restaurant because I personally guaranteed the lease. We started the corporation; we opened a checking account; my money is in there; one other guy's money is in there. And then, the partners who had not put any money in hired the construction company. We got to the restaurant, there was the floor that came from Italy, the chairs, a lot of stuff from Italy.

So, they're building this place and spending a lot of money because we're paying the rent, we're paying the electricity bill, and the money gets low.

The guy that was going to sell the house, he still hasn't sold it, and I made an agreement with him. "I'm going to put up your money, but if you don't repay it by the time we open, I own your share." I didn't use high-powered lawyers for that, I just wrote an agreement. I trusted it would happen; I had no doubts.

So now, I've got $200,000 in. The other partner, he had $80,000, and he didn't have any more money. We were very close to opening; it was February, March, and we ran out of money.

The partners say, "Joe, will you put some more money in?"

I said, "Yes, I'll put more money in, but my percentage is going to go up. My percentage is going to be 28 percent." I put in another $70,000, so now I had $270,000 in.

The partner that I respected, that I thought was honest, he said, "Sure, we'll do that."

I didn't say anything, I didn't do anything. And then, when we really opened, I said we need to have that agreement on paper and he says, "Don't worry about it, take the first profit."

I said, "No, no. We'll share the first profit, and we need to change the agreement on paper, because I put money to get a high percentage." And that's when they started getting shaky.

By this time, I had one guy who didn't put anything in, and I have this agreement since I put my money for his. Nobody else seems to have any money. The two guys from Italy, they made it look like they imported $200,000 worth of equipment. They pay the franchise fee, they say they spent $200,000 for the construction, but in fact the construction guy got screwed because he didn't get paid.

We open after three months, I put in that $270,000; one guy has got $80,000 and he's the same percentage owner as me. The other two people that claim they brought the equivalent with furniture and construction, they're the same as me, too! So, I'm not really happy.

The Italian guys send a cook and one pizza man from Italy, and they have tourist visas, which means they will change every three months because they can't stay longer. And because they can't work here, they wanted us to pay them in cash. I said, no.

Number one, the restaurant doesn't have any cash, and number two, it's illegal to pay in cash. I tell the partners, "You guys hired them, you guys brought them here, you guys pay them in Italy because we can't afford to pay. We're not making any money!"

So now, the pizza guy is not getting paid, the chef is not getting paid, but the company pays for their apartment. And they send a manager from Italy, too, and she's supposed to manage the restaurant, but she has the Italian mentality: "This is the way it's supposed to be. Eat the food. If you don't like it, something's wrong with you."

The pizza was a very good quality. But the pasta, the cook, gets it sent back because it was too *al dente*. The cook says, "Tell them they have to learn how to eat the Italian way." And the waiter says, "I can't tell them that!"

So, customers were not coming back. The name was reputable; a lot of people from the embassies, the World Bank, they're familiar with our name brand, but the restaurant didn't deliver. The pizza men are not getting paid, the chefs are not getting paid, the manager is doing a lousy job. So, the place is paying rent for those three; we pay for their dry cleaning, for the taxi to come to work. Customers want service, quality; they want what they like. People want what they order, they want to enjoy. If they don't enjoy it, they're not coming back.

I guaranteed the lease under my name. And I'm looking at this with my American experience, I can see I'm screwed. So, three months later, I decided to close the restaurant. I reopened it under a different name. My partners sued me. At the same time, I paid the rent every month; I didn't want to default. So, I was paying the rent for about 10 months after the place closed, that's another $100,000, and still another $100,000 for the lawyer.

My partner told me, "If we lose this case, I'm going to come and kill you myself." I got scared. I bought a gun, and I went to the police and said, "This guy is threatening to come and kill me!"

The police says, "Did he kill you yet?"

I said, "No, but he said he would."

The police says, "Well, when he kills you, then we will deal with it." That's what they told me when I went to the station.

And so, fortunately for me, I lost the case. So, I paid them whatever they claimed I owed them. By then I had $700,000 in this place already.

I took legal ownership of the restaurant. I've got to convert the restaurant to il Canale. I put in another $300,000. I really lost count by that time.

I'm thinking "Oh, where will I get the money?" I own real estate, so I was refinancing property and putting money out, stressing on the properties, and also pulled a lot of money out of my house.

I extended the reopening because I changed everything completely. I had to get rid of all their franchise image. I had to repaint, change the wallpaper, floors, art, and so, I guess I'm in about a million dollars in il Canale without it even being opened.

I hired this guy; he was highly recommended as a manager. At the same time, this friend of mine was out of work, and he'd always helped me out. And we hired a wine guy, we had a nice wine list, we had a manager, chef, and everybody started to get on the payroll two or three weeks before we opened.

We planned to open January 2. I told all the employees that we were training. I called a lot of my friends, and we had about 400 people which we served for free for a couple of days. Right after the family and friends, it started snowing. One day, we had three feet of snow.

I had to shut down for a week. I lost half of the people because they didn't show up anymore. They got trained, and they're not making any money. So, I had to hire other people to fill in. I was expecting to be really busy. I hired a public relations firm, which was well-known in the industry, one of the best. That also cost me a couple thousand dollars a month.

The week passed, and we're getting ready to reopen. We wasted a lot of food, but we were preparing, we were ready. The second snowstorm hits! So, what do we do? We shut down again. We shut down for another week or so, and then we open again. I borrowed money from my family, my brother; I sold my pension plans; I liquidated a lot of stuff.

We open around January 12, I think, and everything's calm. I have this manager and assistant manager, and wouldn't you know, they end up being really bad people! The servers and the manager, they turned the restaurant into a party place! I was buying good wine, good liquor; they were drinking, they were stealing. And then, I confront this guy to say, "Hey, you're running a full payroll on 45 percent of the employees!"

He says, "Did you hire me to be a manager, or you want to be the manager?" That's the way he answered me.

I said, "I hired you to be a manager, but we're not doing any numbers compared to the employees that we have. You have a couple of weeks; two, three weeks, you got to chop it down."

He says, "Let me do my job."

He didn't make any change for another couple of weeks, so I told him that I don't need him anymore, I can run the place.

I go back to this gentleman who was a friend of mine for many years before il Canale.

At that time, I was thinking when I might ask him if he wants to work with me because he already had experience.

So I fired the manager who was keeping my payroll 45 percent of what he should have been paying. I called my friend from Miami. I asked him if he wanted to work for me, and he was excited by the idea. He tells me he has a Neapolitan chef and pizza maker that he could bring.

Il Canale was supposed to be a Mediterranean, Neapolitan pizzeria restaurant: no Italian chandeliers or white tablecloths. My friend accepted my job offer and so did the chef.

So, after about two months, I'm changing my kitchen and my management. I am putting in a Neapolitan chef/pizza man and an Italian manager. We had a good cook assistant in the kitchen, and my chef trained him so he could make pizza.

But the sales were not really good; we're doing a couple of thousands a day. In the weekend, we can do $4,000, but really, with that kind of engine, you have a chef and manager, you have taxes and insurance, it's like $16,000 monthly plus all those fixed costs, and the money that was coming in was not enough. I kept putting money in to support the place.

Then April 14, 2010, the waterfront in Georgetown goes underwater because the snow melted in the mountains, and the Potomac river floods. All the waterfront restaurants, four restaurants that people used to go eat for lunch, they close. But my restaurant is open!

By April 15 or 16, we're doubling our sales and my manager calls me, "Joe, something's going on." I knew about that.

I said, "Please try to put extra people on because I think this thing is not going to get fixed right away." We're taking off! By the end of April, the numbers are still climbing, and we didn't stop. First year, I think we did about a million and a half; second year is closer to two million, 1.8 million. Pretty soon we're at three million sales. But that came with a lot of pain, because I've got this big investment in this place and I'm not recovering it yet!

I asked my manager and my chef to help me. I said, "Guys, I'm going to give you ten percent of the profit, but we have to increase sales and cut expenses.

"At the end of the year, I'm going to give you ten percent of the profit each, but we need to make some money. We're not here for fun."

I'm working seven days a week; I ain't making any money personally. Barely surviving. So really, it's not like profit you can pay tax out of. When you pay your credit card, you pay your mortgage, you're done. So, that's like year number three. By year number five, we were doing $3 million, and we began relaxing, but during that time, we got a lot of changes and the restaurant stabilized. The numbers still had to get better even if we're doing better profit. My manager was happy. They're all doing good.

Next door, there was a fish store. The owner closed and I approached the landlord and I said I would like to lease the upstairs because downstairs was too expensive.

He says, "No, Joe. Either you take the whole building or nothing." So, I'm thinking and thinking and thinking, and I said, "Okay." We agreed on a lease and a price and everything. So now, I'm adding another $23,000 on top of $16,000 in monthly rent.

So we have $39,000 a month in rent, plus taxes and insurance. My manager, he was against this expansion. He is hysterical. He had that habit: he would promise to do things, but sometimes he wouldn't follow up; he's behind, overwhelmed. You can't get people like that to change. So, the issues are with my manager; we had two managers, and then one guy left. My chef, he went back home, although he's back with me now. I had to work with the people that I had, that were already trained, which has been a great success. It was amazing. The students became better than the teacher.

So, we're expanding il Canale to next door, which is another 5,000 square feet. I already have about 3,000, so I'm tripling the size. And during this time, there's a lot of stuff going on.

We did it in three phases, the expansion. My manager, by that time, he wasn't very aggressive; he was passive. He wasn't excited, and we got into disagreements. Eventually, the next argument could not be fixed, so he left. Then I hired him back, hoping we could work things out, but he could not agree. There was something going on, and then, finally, I let him go for good. After he left, I decided that all the managers and kitchen workers, the people who don't get tips, should also benefit from profit-shared bonuses.

This other guy was recommended as a manager, but I hired him as a waiter. A month later, I asked him if he wants to step up from being a waiter and be a manager, because I knew he had managing experience.

So now, I got four managers in il Canale, and then I got the chef and the pizza master. They get a big percentage. Then there is the prep, where the assistant chef is getting a nice chunk. And then, it goes down to the dishwasher. So, everybody gets some. And I explained that to Matteo, my new manager, the Italian, and I tell him, "The restaurant is doing very well." I say, "In about six months, we're building a new kitchen, close the old kitchen, and we're going to have 400 seats."

And he says, "I can fill it up. I could do it." He saw that as an opportunity because my other manager was slowing it down. This guy got unleashed. The numbers, they really increased!

The GM, he has a girlfriend. After four years, he gets married. He tells me, "My wife is pregnant, I'm going to go back to Italy."

I say, "What are you doing? Have your baby born here. Make him American." But he wanted him to be born in Florence.

He left two years ago, in June. I asked him if he knew anybody that he could recommend, and he recommended a manager who was pretty good. That manager lasted a year and helped us get through COVID. Then I asked my son, Alessandro, who'd been working at the restaurant three years. "Do you want to hire another GM?"

He says, "No, Dad I can do the job."

I'm always taking it one day at a time because you never know when staff are going to have another opportunity to follow their dreams. This business is tough. You train your people, you give them everything you've got, but it's natural for them to move on.

Now I've got general manager number four, which is my son.

Seventeen

The way A Modo Mio is structured is pretty much like any other restaurant. We structure based on what we need. We want to go faster, we want to pick up the speed for service. So, the kitchen prepares the food, then there's the foot runners, who monitor and see which order is ready and make sure it's the whole order, and then they pick it up.

The busses clean and spray the tables and all the items there, including the chairs. We're used to doing the whole cleaning, and since COVID we're using disinfectants. The servers, they take the orders. They should be there when the order comes in and put them on the customer's table. Keep the water full, keep the wine glasses full, keep the beer full. Make sure the customers have everything they need—salt and pepper shakers, oil, oregano, and cheese. If they need anything, like an extra napkin, the waiter is there. That's what I see. I tell them to make sure that wherever you are in the restaurant, whatever you do, always try to have eye contact with your table and let them know that you're there; never turn your back on your customers. You want to see your station all the time, so the customers, if for some reason they need something, they don't have to wave to get your attention. The customer knows that you're watching him, so you get his attention right away.

We're a casual restaurant, so a waiter has a minimum of five, six, sometimes ten tables. It depends on the night, and it depends on the waiter, the waitress, and the server. There are servers that can handle ten tables and there are servers that can't.

When I hire a server, I usually ask, "Have you been a waitress before or a server?" If they have, I ask them what level? Because there are servers, they work only breakfasts. Or maybe they work at a spareribs place or it's at pizza. So, I try to figure out what kind of experience they have. I ask them why they left. How are they going to get to work? Do they have another job?

Also, were they full-time or part-time? Full-time, they do maybe four- or five-night shifts and couple of lunch shifts, usually. Some of them want three-four nights, and some they work only four nights, and others work only lunch. You want to ask a lot of questions. Did they go to school? Do they have kids?

I will hire perfect waiters. The good waiters that will have experience. They'll be available when I want them, and they know what to do. There's some conflict, like, "Oh, I can only work three days a week, Wednesday, Thursday, Monday." It's like, that's already complicated enough. I don't want to complicate it more. We don't want to force their life to change for us, but at the same time, we don't want the restaurant to change for them. So, we're trying to protect the restaurant first and see if this employee, if we add him to the schedule, will he improve what we have, or will he hurt it? I'm trying to make sure that when we make a move, the person we hire makes things better.

Usually, it's a general manager that hires the servers. I hire the GM, chef, and the pizza chef. And they hire the rest of the kitchen staff. My job is to work with the heads of the restaurant, and I don't want to keep track of everybody. It's difficult for me. I want to lead them and shape them the way I want.

With a GM, I'll ask the same questions. Where do you live? Are you married? Are you single? You go to the gym? Do you play sports? Where did you work before? I mean, these are very social questions. You want to know what kind of human being you are dealing with. I want to see how they answer those questions. And they have to be honest about it; I have to feel the honesty. I let them explain themselves, what they know about the job. They tell me what they've been doing, where they worked, and what they're really good at.

There are some people who are good with their hands; some are good with the personnel; others are good with ideas, or with the technical; and others, still, are good with promotions. Everyone has their own niche.

What's their gift? I make sure they communicate clearly, so other people can understand them. I want them to know when they can make a judgment about some situation, on an emergency, or under stress.

I ask if they are a server or waiter or manager, "What kind of experience you have with wine and beer? If you are an order taker, do you make suggestions?

"If you're a waiter, what happens if your foot runners and your buses don't show up."

If he says, "Well, yes, then I clean the tables." That's what I want. And as a manager, if they say, "If my cooks are not here, I close the restaurant…"

One time I had a manager, a GM, and the computer wasn't working. It was just a cash register. He closed the restaurant, but he kept all the employees inside, so they were on the payroll; the waiter, the cooks, and everybody. I was like, "If you're going to close the doors, send everybody home, so at least you cut the expenses. You don't keep the clock going, and you don't let a customer in…"

Well, you go manual, you get some checks. I have a system in case the computer crashes. I use a calculator and get checks. This used to happen 20, 30 years ago. The new system, those things don't crash anymore,

I used to get my pizza chefs from Italy. But there's a lot of legal and immigration issues with that, unless they're stars, unless a chef has a lot of articles in newspapers. Then they can get special visas. I used to get them in Italy and bring them here. There were always issues where they couldn't work. And if they did, then they were like kings, princes. They'll make pizza. That's all they did. For me, a pizza man needs to keep the station sparkling, clean, and organized. He needs to prepare and have a uniform. Some of the chefs from Italy were really sloppy. Maybe one out of two or three were good, but the other ones are lazy, they smoked. I decided to train my own pizza makers.

Now I'll get some guy who already knows the basics, and I'll train him. I put him in as an assistant. He does the vegetables, he cuts the meat, and he cleans the area and the machines. And slowly but surely, he'll start making pizzas, he'll start putting the toppings.

Also, the oven is very important because we're working with the wood or gas oven and the pizza cooks in a minute, a minute-and-a-half. So, if you have five, six, seven pizzas in the oven, you got to know how to manage them.

So they're apprentices. If they're young, and they are sharp, and they're aggressive, they can start making pizza in a couple of months. Then we put them in at the end of the day or the beginning of the day when the restaurant is slow.

Anyway, that's the most important thing. You can hire people for any position, any position at all. Most of the people who don't have experience and open a restaurant, they make mistakes. You're the owner, or you're cook, you're manager, you're helper, you have maybe five, six people in the kitchen. Then one person leaves, and the restaurant goes tilt. You want somebody to fill that position right away. But I think it's best to wait, even if just a couple of days. You divide the work; the manager maybe takes over that position before he fills it. It's best to wait until you find someone, and you can understand each other. You ask some questions, and you get the right answers. You can communicate. "Can you show up right now?"

If a server worked in other restaurants, they'll bring all the problems that happened at the other restaurant and get everybody confused. You get stressed, and sometimes the new person gets pissed off and leaves right then and there. But if you take your time explaining to the new employees what they're going to do, they'll go where they have to go. Walk them through the restaurant. Or let's say if it's a dishwasher, show them where the chemicals are, where the brushes are, where the trays are. Where are the menus, the glasses, the plates, where are the napkins, the forks and knives, everything?

So, when they come in, you do that, and in a couple of days they get used to it. The best is to hire people when you're growing, so you will not have an emergency when one person goes missing. You are doing good, you are thinking, "You know what? Let's bring another person in because we are getting busy." You do that instead of building that person into that position. You have to open yourself to grow versus closing yourself and limiting yourself.

With a new server, what we do first is we'll put him with another server to see what they do. They'll do that for a couple of shifts so you get to see how they work.

After a couple of days, we'll give the new person a menu, and we tell them to start getting familiar with the foods. Go with the pizza, then drink, lunch, beers. You get familiar working with the server, and you get familiar with the table, the numbers, where the bathrooms are, where the bar is, where the exit and entrance are. You get familiar with your space.

The menu doesn't really change much. We have some specials, we take them off the menu, and we put them back on request. We're going to test you on the menu. We are going to sit down with you and then go through the menu and say, "Well, what's Burrata? Because, yes, it's fresh Burrata." But if you don't know or say what it is, we'll explain what the Burrata is.

So, they have to know the menu. They have to know what's there. It takes six or seven days before they start taking orders from the tables. It's just like a team and that's their position. The manager is the quarterback, and the GM is the coach.

The servers, they are pretty much the first contact with guests. If the waiter is good, and the food is good, the customers are going to be happy; they're going to have a good experience because the waiter represented the restaurant well, and the customers will return.

On the third day we'll have the assistant, the new person, starting and taking on some of the server's work; they do it together. They'll take the order together, and they are both taking notes. Each one greets the customer when they come in. The older server maybe asks the guest, "What would you like? Do you like this or that?" The new server hears the question and takes notes. When they finish taking the order, if there's no question, the new server should have learned something.

Then they go to the terminals and learn to put in the order. That's another part of the job, learning how to operate that system. They have their own card to open the terminal so no one can open or close their check.

So, when the new person has been there for a few days, we start scheduling an interview for the menu. Normally it's on the fifth day, though sometimes there are delays.

The manager does that. On those days, the manager puts the

new person with the other server, and one of the managers will sit down with the new person and start to ask questions. What's this? What's that? Where's table number 61? The key questions that people or customers ask when they order a pizza, what do you say? Because we serve a Neapolitan pizza, and it's sort of a new thing in the USA. You tend to get a different kind of pizza here. Our pizza, it cannot be made crispy. Even if you're cooking in the oven and it gets burned, it doesn't get crispy. The oven is really hot, about 900 degrees, so the dough stays tender. There's a lot of water in the dough, and the heat of the oven does not have a chance to dry it out, so it's just soft, juicy, and tender.

So, we have a saying that when new customer comes in, and they've never eaten our pizza before, it's a rule of the restaurant that we tell them to forget anything they know about pizza and start over from scratch. Because otherwise they have expectations of what pizza has been like. In Naples, the pizza is different. We prepare the guests for what they're going to get.

Sometimes some of the servers won't do well in the test. So, we'll say, "Okay. Go back with the waiter." We're trying not to put them on the floor because we want them to represent in the best way possible.

And then, when we do put them on the floor, we don't start them with 10 tables, we start them with two tables, three tables. If they're good, then four tables. If they have issues for a couple of weeks, they don't know this, they don't know that, it usually isn't going to work out.

There's only three times when I recommend letting people go. One is when they steal, one is when they harass co-workers, and when they don't do their job. We give a written warning, and they sign it. If they repeat the behavior, they get fired.

The thing is in America, we don't have restaurant schools. We have chef school, we don't have schools for waiters to teach how to prepare the dining room, serve the dinner up, or how to take orders. In Europe, there are schools for that.

We have an issue because here, being a waiter, it's a stepping-stone. You'd do it for a couple of years, and then you do something else, and you move on. In the high-end restaurant, the really high end, they do it as a career. But in our level of restaurant, most of the people do it because they are going to school, or they're waiting for another job. Some, they last between five, six, seven years, it depends. Some get married. I mean, a lot of stuff happens in the five, six years that they work there.

All told, I have maybe 50 or 60 employees.

We're actually one of the fortunate restaurants; we were able to keep our teams. But if you go out to any other restaurants, they probably have half the staff, and some restaurants closed because they don't have enough staff. We were fortunate. Since the D.C. government put back 100 percent occupancy, the business has peaked, it's increased by 20 percent to date.

We are building up, and I did something a little bit creative to get waiters, servers, and people in the kitchen at all levels. I told everybody in the kitchen, if you bring somebody that you know and who works for us at least three months, I'll give you a $500 bonus. And because I need more waiters, I told all the waiters and all the managers, if they bring a server, a waiter, or a waitress, and if that person stays more than three months, I'll give them $1,000. Usually, good workers know good workers. Good people know good people. And they'll be able to move up, hopefully the next couple of weeks or a month.

Eighteen

Il Canale's been open since 2010, and we've had a lot of famous guests that came through. The first was Vincent Gray, the ex-mayor of Washington. He announced his campaign to run for mayor in il Canale in February, 2010. That was just a month after we opened. We had Dan Marino dining here. We had the actor Mike Lowe and the singer Michael Bolton. We served Harrison Ford.

One time the White House reserved one side of the restaurant and the Trumps came, Ivanka and Jared Kushner. That night we served over 100 guests and a lot of journalists. We've had Nancy Pelosi and the Obama daughters. That was about the same time Hillary Clinton came and ate here. I wasn't here that day, but I would have been excited to meet her!

We had Tony Renis, who wrote "Quando Quando Quando." The Italian Wounded Warriors usually are my guests here every year. When famous people come, we ask if we can take their photos, and then we frame the pictures and put them on the walls. Actually, I don't have enough wall space. I have a spare room full of photos...

Carl Reiner came with a bunch of people, producers and stars you read about, and they drank a lot of wine from our cantina.

We have s special relationship with Luciano Gennaro, who owns Porto Alba, the oldest pizza place in Naples. He came in here and shared information.

The news anchor Anderson Cooper came to dine with friends.

My neighbor and friend, Italo Rodriguez, who owns the little hotel next door, he brought the President of Portugal, and they had cappuccino.

Steven Tyler was here when his band came to play a concert downtown on the Mall.

Then one day Ligabue, a rockstar in Italy, came with his wife and his manager. One of my staff, she was the star of the restaurant, she recognized him. She went to the manager and said, "Well, we got Ligabue here!"

In 2018, we were chosen among the 70 best pizzeria and restaurant in the world by Ristorazione Italiana Magazine. That was spectacular!

Yelp named us one of the top hundred restaurants in America. We were number 40.

We've had so many famous people at the restaurant, that a lot of customers who have never been here before, they take a tour, like a museum. Really, il Canale has become a landmark!

We've had so many awards it's hard to remember them all!

Nineteen

There are a lot of frustrations, like when you confront some people because they think they know, but they don't know that they don't know. You're trying to tell them your vision, you're trying to tell them the way you see it, it's like talking to a deaf person.

I've come in when the place should be open, and it isn't. Or the Open sign isn't turned on. That drives me crazy! I'm talking to the person in charge, and he says, "Oh yes, I know. Yes, I know..."

I don't give a shit if he knows, or if he doesn't know. This is a business. You open it 11 o'clock, you put your Open sign on, your air-condition should be ready, all the tables should be set, the door should be clean, etc. Everything should be done!

And then I try so many approaches. So, the frustration is that I try to move, talking about outside of the restaurant, the inside of the restaurant, before working, during working. One day, I came in A Modo Mio and wanted to see what's up, why the numbers have plateaued here every Friday and Saturday. They get to a place, and they stop. But I don't think it's because of the customers; it's because of my staff. Let's say if we do $5,000 in sales, and the staff get ready for that. And when they make $7,000, they go into the weeds because they're not ready. So, I'm here recently, I'm trying to get them ready to go to $10,000, and I get resistance from my chef and from my manager. They think I'm asking too much. I mean, if you're not ready when the rush comes, you'll fail!

The staff had a whole day to get ready for this. You're busy because you're setting up now, instead of taking care of preparations earlier. It's like you're losing the war already. You're never going to increase those numbers!

I am coming here and saying, buy the tools, prepare what you need, and they say, "Yes, yes, yes, yes." And I come in and the stations and the prep are not complete. I'm here trying to get them going on Friday night because I figured we'll go to seven, we'll go to eight, because we have the capacity, and we have the customers.

My staff is one of the reasons why we don't go up with the numbers. If it gets too busy, they turn the delivery off. The servers have no time to give a check, or ask, "Do you want another glass of wine?" So, it's very frustrating for me because I've opened many restaurants, and A Modo Mio is eight months old. By now it should be like a Swiss watch.

You should have everything clicking. You should be ready, because the business is sort of like this: if you prepare, you succeed. If you're not prepared, you're going to go into the weeds. When you go into the weeds, your sales stop. And I know it's not just sales, it's the goodwill of the customers, and the service, and the atmosphere. Then the customers look at you like you're stupid and don't know what you're doing!

One day, I remember, I asked the chef, "When are you going to be ready for 10,000?" I was pushing him. At the time, I was cutting bread, because the bread was hot. I put it in a refrigerator to cool it off before I cut it, and my chef was arguing with me. "Why did you put the bread in the refrigerator? You are losing quality." It's sort of like, he knows better, like I'm trying to hurt quality, and he's trying to protect it. So he's protecting quality, but he's hurting the service.

How do you get through that? I think it's really hard to have people change.

A lot of the time I choose the wrong people, and I have the idea that they're going to change. It's really hard because a lot of people are coming from different cultures. Say you have a culture that's from Italy. I'm thinking that we had a culture that's good, Catholic, hardworking, principled people. But at the same time, we are a culture that's been dominated by the wealthy. It's like the lower class, it does not move. They've stopped. In Italy, I see the people that I went to school with. They've become teachers or whatever. They just did not improve or make any progress in the culture and in getting better. I mean, they're great people, but they're not really changing because the generation before, the generation before that, and the generation before that, it's the same.

Maybe they're eating different food, maybe they're dressing different, maybe they have modern houses. But really, they just stopped when they got the necessities.

What's the necessity? What's in style? What's in this modern time? It seems like they can't see it. I think it's ingrained. I don't want to sound like I changed it by myself, I know that's not true. Maybe something in America changed me because I started realizing what I don't know. When I started to become teachable, everything opened up.

The most frustrated thing is when you're working with family, special people, and you have higher expectations. Then you have different kinds of people who come in, and they know that they don't know, and they learn so beautifully. When I have people who say, "Oh, I know how to do everything," I say "What's everything?"

I'd rather they not hide what they don't know. I'd rather have someone say, "Well, I've never worked in this job before, but I'm willing to learn." And I can teach them because they're coming from a place they don't know.

And even the pizza man I had here a long time, it just didn't work because we changed concept, and he kept doing the same thing.

I wanted him to dance to a different beat, but he danced to the same beat as before. He just did what he already knew; he couldn't see it. And I'm trying to tell him what will make the job easier and faster and more efficient. That's the frustration that I have every day.

Owning a restaurant is one of the most dangerous businesses. The chance of success is very small. They say that every hundred restaurants that open, half of them, they close by the first year or two, and the other half, 25 percent of those barely make it and meet expenses. And then, you're left with the other 25 percent, of which half pay a salary to their owners. So now you are you left with the other 12 percent, where maybe 10 percent of them make a good living, and then two or three percent of those are making good money, excellent money. So the chance of really making a lot of money in the restaurant business is like three to five percent. Almost any other business has a better chance to succeed, a bigger chance.

If you sell shoes, let's say, you have a good chance that if you opened a shoe store, if the location is right, you can make a lot of money, because you're buying for a dollar and selling for two dollars. However, in the restaurant business, you're buying flours, and you're buying tomatoes, and you're buying a lot of cheese, and you're buying bulk spaghetti, and then you're serving the dish hot and warm with fresh *parmigiano* and fresh basil. So, there's really a lot going on at the same time. And it's like you're building a team, there are a lot of moving parts. Real estate, taxes, electricity, gas, you got that going on, you have the accounting going on and the employees going. You have management, cleaning, and on and on and on. All those moving parts, some of them are getting ignored, the other ones you get right.

I come in and the table was dirty; somebody missed cleaning it. They missed a step to wash the table, right? If you missed a step in the kitchen, it gets to the table and it's wrong, now what?

It's like dominos, and if you're not quick enough to catch it, sometimes the customer has to tell you. Most restaurant owners, they think they're right. So, when a customer complains, they say, "What's he complaining about?"

If I catch it, I catch it by putting my finger in the sauce, putting my finger in the boiling water, go to the refrigerator, check the temperature, see how long the food has been prepared. Check the day when you got delivery, check the day when you use it. Check the temperature of the air conditioner in the dining room. It's all natural to me; I walk in I can feel it if the air conditioner is working; I can feel if it doesn't work, even if it's a little off. If I open the refrigerator, I can feel the temperature; I could tell if the refrigerator is fine or not. So, a lot of that stuff comes from the experience I got through 50 years doing it...

It's the same thing with real estate, choosing a location. You can choose a location, and let's say you can sell a million dollars, and then you choose another location, and you can sell $2 million without changing anything. Sometimes, you can do $4 million.

This stuff is complicated, lots of moving parts. Entrepreneurship requires vision. You have to see the deal through without emotions and trust your guts.

Let me give you an example.

Right now, I've got a LOI (Letter of Intent), which is an offer to open restaurants. I'm gonna have an LOI in Naples, Florida. We've been working for about two months, three months, trying to look for the right place. We knocked on a lot of doors, and we made a lot of phone calls. We met with a lot of landlords, and after everything, what we've got going on right now, we have a place that is really better than all the others because this is location, location, location. So, this location, we have to buy a restaurant that is not doing the right amount of numbers of sales. So, these people, they built a great restaurant in the best location of Naples, Florida, but for some reason, it's not doing what they wanted, so they want to sell it.

It's the management most likely. If the location is right, it's the management. The owner, maybe he's been successful in other restaurants and in this one he missed it; maybe he missed the menu, the concept and it's not working the way he expected. So, I think he's paying over $250,000 a year rent, and his sales are less than $2 million, which is not good. The numbers don't work.

We've bet on the place, and I think we should be able to do $3 million or $3.5 million if we do our concept. So, the numbers work better, but let's keep our fingers crossed on what we're going to do. I'm depending on my guy, my partner, who is the champion pizza maker, and he's got a good sense of business. We're going to plan the menu, the concept and hopefully, it'll work. If we do the $3.5 million or $4 million, that means we'll be among the top 10 percent of restaurants. If we do $3 million or $3.5 million, then we'll be among the 10 to 15 percent. If we do $2 million, then we will be the other 50 percent, and we won't be profitable.

So, what's involved are guarantees. Landlords, they don't just give you a property for you to put in a restaurant without guarantees. And because we don't have any recognition in Naples, they want a personal guarantee. I have to give them my financials and my tax return, so they can see that if something goes wrong, they can get their rent for whatever time we agree to guarantee. Most likely, there's two years, maybe three. Probably they'll go down to one year after the third or fourth year, and then going to one year or six months. And after a while, we switch to the corporation, and the restaurant will be the guarantor. So, when the corporation becomes successful, you are on the hook for three or four years, the landlord wants guaranteed rent.

We're going to propose leasing with option to buy for that particular situation, because it's on a major street in Naples, which is among the most expensive real estate in the country. It's like being in Georgetown in Washington, or on Fifth Avenue in New York.

The owners won't sell. I would like to go with at least a five-year lease, and four-, five-years options. That gives us an opportunity to go in, try it for five years, and if it doesn't work, not renew. So, you don't guarantee anything if it doesn't work, and you get off the train. But if you're doing good, you have the option to renew for five years, and then if you continue to do good, you renew again. I'd like to go that way. My intuition is to go even more because I want to bet to succeed. If I have a 30-years guarantee to do that, someday I could sell the business, and the people that buy it, they'd also have time to make their money. But the landlords don't like that. In some cases, they might, it depends if you're small, or if they like to keep the property busy, keep it rented all the time, and you guarantee a rent. Some landlords, depending on if they have prime real estate, they know if you don't make it, somebody else can make it, so every time they change renter, they get more rent.

The thing is, you write a LOI and you're trying to buy a business that is not making any money. The seller is trying to sell it because he's losing money, but the landlord doesn't care because he receives rent from the loser's business. But at the same time, in his gut, he knows that the guy can't pay rent forever if he doesn't make any money. That's where the frustration is.

The guy that is selling the restaurant, he knows he has a good location so he's trying to hold onto his price. I have to give him a good enough offer for him to sell. And then, we're going to go to the landlord, and the thing about it is if my credit is good—which it is—the landlord will accept it, along with the old terms.

Where we're buying, the price of a square foot a few years ago was almost half the price it is now. So we might be able to make a deal with the seller of this restaurant that is losing money, but we might not be able to make a deal with the landlord.

Usually, in the lease, there is a clause that says if I qualify, we can assume the years left in the lease for the same price. So, the landlords have to accept. They know what they have, and they know that if you're successful, you make a lot of money; they want to get a piece of it. Negotiating, that's the challenge right now.

That's an example I wanted to give you. In this particular case, the landlord did not like our concept, and he turned us down.

Twenty

I spend my time preventing disasters. This is pretty much what I do all day. When I walk around any of the restaurants, I see what's wrong.

Let's talk about electricity. I make sure that if I see an uncovered wire or a plug that is not functioning, that doesn't look right, or loose wires people have walked on, or hit, or moved, it's like I'm the only one that sees that stuff. I have somebody in the restaurant who does my equipment maintenance. He cleans all the filters and does all that handyman work. So, if I tell him to do what's needed without my getting involved, then things work better, and the job gets done.

Then the technician says, "You have to keep this space clear," and believe me, it's clear all the time. I leave it a couple of weeks, I come back, and there's some stuff in the way. And I take pictures and send it to the restaurant management. They say, "I got it."

Sometimes, the ice machine starts acting out, and equipment that's acting out, I can sort of feel it. And I say, "Do that," and they do it and then they forget about it. Then, you've got to follow up, and call the technician and see to it the job is complete and keep a log of the work done. It's better now than it used to be, but it's still not perfect. Unfortunately, you can't always trust the contractors. They cut corners if you don't watch them and follow up.

Recently, the ice machine at il Canale broke a couple of days before the weekend. We have three ice machines; one is on the top floor, and I had ordered my manager to turn it on, but for some reason he couldn't do it because the breaker was off, and he left it off. So, then, here we go, we're going to go out and buy ice. So, we have to go out, buy ice, break it, and it's all this extra work that I'm trying to prevent. The refrigerator has to be at the right temperature, but the thermostat inside is wrong. And I say, "No, I want this refrigerator at 34 degrees, but the temperature is 37 because the thermostat is not functioning. So, I put in another thermostat there, and let's check. Yeah, the thermostat checks at 34.

Sometimes I feel I am constantly complaining. I say the music doesn't sound healthy; there's too much bass. I'm saying, "Can you fix it? You know how to do it?"

They say, "I know how to do that." But then, why didn't they fix it without me pointing it out? I mean, if it's done electronically, you can adjust it with your phone. It makes the music a little clearer and not boom, boom, boom, and nobody hears that.

The air conditioner was broken, and they said, "No, it's not broken." It was a fight to prove that it was. I'm preventing things from deteriorating.

Maybe I built this business so big that it's hard to control.

So, I'm a little bit burned out because at this point, I'm leaving, and I'm going to be gone for seven weeks, and I wanted to do a lot of the stuff so everyone could work comfortably. I'm concerned that if something goes wrong now, and they can't prevent it, it'll take longer to fix.

But how do you hire a personal assistant? For example, my four bank accounts got hacked about two months ago, and I had to open four new accounts. But the other accounts are still open because there're deposits going in. And who do I send to the bank? An assistant?

I have been in this position forever; I think I'm just realizing that I've been doing fine. Now I'm motivating. This is just swirling around me, and my job has been getting bigger and bigger, and busier and busier.

I'm checking the windows, the bathrooms, the air conditioner, the music, everything, and building a new restaurant. Those guys that work for me, they run the restaurant, they should be able to do that. Some days, it feels like they don't do things right, and I have to tell them again and again or do it myself.

You'd think after more than 50 years in this business, you have finally arrived, but it's only a daily reprieve. You realize it's a day-to-day commitment. When you open the doors, the game is on, and everybody needs to play together, like a soccer team or a band. Sometimes the music is spectacular, sometimes it's chaos.

For me, I have to accept this is the way it is and give it my best shot, knowing my team is doing the best it can. Tomorrow is another day.

So, my thinking is that when I come back from Italy, I'm going to reevaluate. Maybe I need somebody with bigger balls.

My broker, he says, "Joe, you have other things to do. You need somebody to coordinate all this stuff."

The guy who's going to coordinate the builder and everything for the 90 Second Pizza? He said, "Yeah." Thank God there's people that can do that because I'm usually coordinating everything by myself.

I am worried about leaving. Because I usually leave, and every time I do, at il Canale, there's an experienced GM. Now it's my son that's stepped up, and he's been doing it for a little while. The whole team is good, very good as a team, but my son is new in charge. I reminded him that it's not heart surgery, what he's doing. He just needs to keep the fires going, that's all. Maybe he sees me stressed, and he gets stressed too. That could be it.

We're going to Italy in the summer. We'll be back in D.C. for the fall, and then we'll go to Florida. What I want is to enjoy my family, and what I'm going to do, really, is pretty much nothing. Just sleep and take a nap in the afternoon. Eat good and say nothing, do nothing.

But really, I'm not going to do nothing. I'm going to keep doing what I love, building and growing!

I've had a good life with a lot of satisfaction. My sons, my wife and her daughters, all love me. I'm thankful for all I have. I was born in Sicily and grew up in the United States. I am a Sicilian American Pizza Man. It's the best of both worlds.

ACKNOWLEDGEMENTS

Family

My father and my mother, Rosario and Maria Farruggio, for giving me pride and faith.

My sister, Maria Farruggio and her husband, Fortunato; my brother Vincenzo and his wife Rosa; my brother Lillo and his wife, Maria; and all their families, for standing by me and teaching me patience, love, and endurance.

My former wife, Mariolina Barba, who gave me my wonderful sons.

My three sons, Roberto, who has given me joy and showed me how to endure pain; Enrico, for his sweetness and finding his path; and Alessandro, who has taught me balance in all things.

My wife Teresa, who since we met has enriched my life and made me happier and stronger than I have ever been, and her daughters Dalila and Manuela, who love me and have given me patience, and let me see life through their eyes.

My aunt Giuseppina, the first to suggest I learn the pizza business.

My uncle Luigi Agliata, who like a father taught me respect.

Friends

My friends from childhood, including Rosario Aquista and Antonio Chiarelli who were generous, encouraging and proud of me.

Lillo Carlino, my first partner, who believed in me.

The people of Castrofilippo, my town, who in my worst time would not let me fail.

Pat Tenorio, who encouraged me to become an entrepreneur and trusted me from the beginning.

Giuseppe Sedita, a friend in the best and worst of times.

Pino Castiglione, a shining example of how to run marathons.

Angelo Taibi, a friend and confidant.

Advisors

Kevin Sullivan, who showed me what was possible and what was not.

E. David Harrison, my attorney and personal advisor.

Vittorio Rosso, a friend and the first General Manager of Il Canale.

Antonio Biglietto, my chef and maestro of the Neapolitan pizza and Southern Italian cuisine.

Carlo Anibal Salvatierra Lopez, a master pizza chef.

Miguel Guevara, a chef who exceeded all my expectations.

Idalia Maldonado, always dependable and solid as a rock.

Roberto Farruggio, my talented son who designed the logos for Il Canale and A Modo Mio.

Giorgio Greco, who had boundless energy on which I could depend and trust.

Melo Cicala, who designed and built Il Canale and continues to coach me.

Barbara Hawthorn, who did the original interior design of Il Canale.

Janet Staihar, who put Il Canale on the map.

Hugh McGee, a friend, graphic designer and promoter of Mamma Maria's, Joe's Place, JoJo Pizza Buffet, and 90 Second Pizza.

Matteo Russoniello, my second General Manager who took us from a mom-and-pop restaurant to a mainstream establishment.

My son Alessandro, who since 2021 has been Il Canale's General Manager.

Jacob Middel, my broker who taught me that time will erase all real estate mistakes.

Abdul Mouhssine, who is both humble and professional.

Bruno Conti, an energetic and precise colleague.

Paolo Buffa, there from the very beginning.

Enlightenment

I cannot say enough about all the people who were there for me and helped me understand how to live my life one day at a time while encouraging my ambitions. You know who you are, and all have a place in my heart.

I am sure that I have not named all the family and friends who have enriched my life by example. By crossing my path, you have helped me build, and are still helping. You have my undying gratitude.

I will always be grateful for America, the country that adopted me and my family, and gave us everything we have.

My mother and father, Maria and Rosario, in 1971.

Alessandro high school graduation.

Rome Marathon, 2004.

My son Alessandro and I in Italy.

Venice, Italy.

An American Story

Roberto, Enrico and Alessandro in Virginia, 1999.

Nephews and nieces in Castrofilippo, 1998. From left to right, Pietro, Alessandro, Giorgia, Clelia, Floriana, Roberto.

My mother Maria in a Sicilian vineyard.

Old friends competing in a non-profit golf tournament. From left to right, Hugh, Mike, me, and John.

With my friend Ennio and my niece Patrizia at Joe's Pizza and Pasta in Gaithersburg, MD.

Ocean City with Roberto, July 1989.

My three sons are a handful!

An American Story 189

The first Joe's Place, Pizza and Subs, Woodbridge, 1978.

Front row, left to right: Me, my brother Vinney and my cousin Steve.
Back row, left to right: My cousin Maria, Vinney's wife Rosa, my wife Teresa, and her daughter Dalila.

My brothers Calogero and Vincenzo.

il Canale's oven, imported from Napoli.

Christmas dinner with family and friends at il Canale.

With singer and songwriter Tony Renis.

Day two at 90 Second Pizza in Georgetown with my running friends.

Left: I grow basil and roses on il Canale's rooftop.
Right: My nephew Pietro at the original 90 Second Pizza in Georgetown.

After winning 4th place for the best Neapolitan pizza in the world at the Las Vegas Pizza Expo.

The Georgetown University Soccer Team a week before the championship. When they won, I treated them at il Canale.

Teresa and I on our wedding day.

A tender moment.

After the wedding in City Hall, with my family.

Columbus Day in D.C. with fellow Italian Americans, Melo, Francesco, me, my wife, and Pino.

My friend Italo Rodriguez and I in il Canale's Fiat 500.

Painting of il Canale's Fiat 500.

The Farruggio family comes to il Canale for a holiday dinner.

The Wall of Fame to il Canale's second floor.

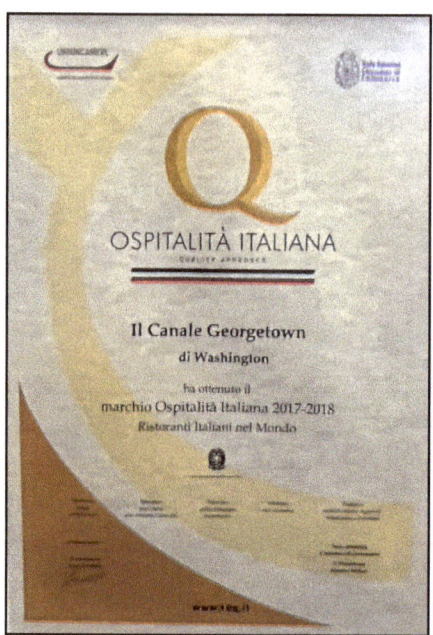

Ospitalita Italiana said il Canale was one of the best Italian restaurants in the world.

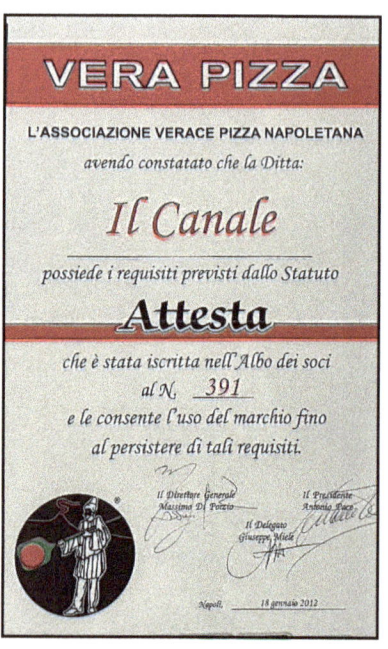

The Association of True Neapolitan Pizza says we are the real thing!

The Robert Facchina Italian American Museum of Washington, D.C. named il Canale one of the legendary Italian restaurants in the Nation's Capital.

The *Travel and Leisure* magazine award.

Yelp liked us too!

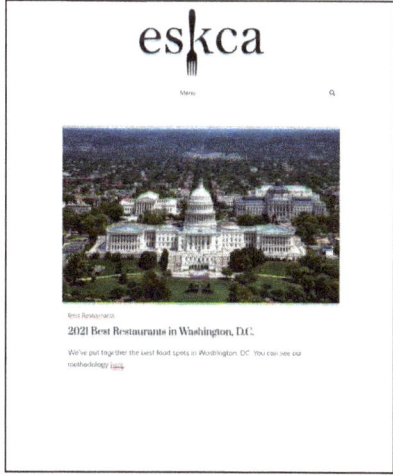

The ESKCA Award for top restaurant in D.C.

My wonderful wife with me as we receive the 70 Best Restaurants with Pizzeria in the World award.

The Gambero Rosso Award for top Italian Restaurant.

Hillary Clinton enjoys a pizza at il Canale.

I had the honor of serving Brigitte Macron, the First Lady of France.

An American Story

President Trump's Press Secretary, Sarah Sanders, now Governor of Arkansas.

Kellyanne Conway, Counselor to President Trump.

Joe Coleman, lead singer of The Platters, and his wife.

Queen Latifa comes for dinner.

Rock star Steven Tyler drops in before a non-profit concert at the George Washington Memorial.

Harrison Ford and Alessandro.

Patrick Stewart with Alessandro Farruggio (left) and Matteo Rusoniello (right).

James Comey, former FBI Director.

Sometimes even American historical figures want great Neopolitan fares!

Woody Harrelson
with il Canale's General Manager.

Jared and Ivanka Trump.

Actor/singer Mandy Patinkin
with Vittorio Rosso,
the first il Canale General Manager.

Jay Leno lunches at il Canale.

The unmistakable Conan O'Brian.

Mr. Michael Bolton
with il Canale's hostess, Rosalia.

My runner friends came from Italy to D.C. to run the National Marathon.

I am The Pizza Man! With Angelo, John, and Holly at the New York Marathon.

About Thierry Sagnier

Thierry Sagnier is a writer whose works have been published in the United States and abroad. He is the author of *The IFO Report*, (Avon Books), *Bike! Motorcycles and the People who Ride Them* (Harper & Row) and *Washington by Night* (Washingtonian Books). He is also the author of *Thirst*, a thriller based in Washington, DC's, mean streets, and the sequel, *Dope*. *Writing about People, Places and Things* is a collection of essays chronicling Sagnier's thoughts on writing, family and friendships, and cancer.

In 2016 he wrote *The Fortunate Few*, recounting the memories of the men and women who served with the International Voluntary Services, the precursor of the Peace Corps. *Montparnasse*, a novel set in Paris shortly after World War I, was published by Apprentice Press in April, 2019. He is currently working in a sequel to his novel *L'Amérique*, as well as on a sequel to *Dope*.

Sagnier was born in France and came to the United States in his early teens. He has worked and written for *The Washington Post* and several other newspapers and magazines, produced videos and short films for the Canadian Broadcasting Corporation, and was a columnist for Canada's *Le Devoir*. He was Senior Writer for the World Bank and traveled the world to write about that institution's projects in developing countries.

His plays have been produced both nationally and internationally, notably by Tada Theater in New York. They were also featured in the East End Fringe Festival.

He currently lives in Virginia.

www.ingramcontent.com/pod-product-compliance
Lightning Source LLC
Chambersburg PA
CBHW061727070526
44583CB00024B/3042